John Charles Thorowgood

The climatic treatment of consumption and chronic lung diseases

John Charles Thorowgood

The climatic treatment of consumption and chronic lung diseases

ISBN/EAN: 9783337731199

Printed in Europe, USA, Canada, Australia, Japan

Cover: Foto ©ninafisch / pixelio.de

More available books at **www.hansebooks.com**

THE
CLIMATIC TREATMENT

OF

CONSUMPTION

AND

CHRONIC LUNG DISEASES

BY

JOHN C. THOROWGOOD, M.D., LOND.,

MEMBER OF THE ROYAL COLLEGE OF PHYSICIANS OF LONDON;
ASSISTANT-PHYSICIAN TO THE CITY OF LONDON HOSPITAL
FOR DISEASES OF THE CHEST, VICTORIA PARK;
PRESIDENT OF THE WEST KENT MEDICO-
CHIRURGICAL SOCIETY, AND LATE
PHYSICIAN TO ROYAL GEN-
ERAL DISPENSARY.

A Third, and Enlarged Edition,

Of the Author's Work on Change of Air in the Prevention and Cure of Consumption, with a Chapter on the Diet and Regimen of Pulmonic Invalids.

LONDON:
H. K. LEWIS, 136 GOWER STREET, W.C.
1868.

PREFACE.

———o———

The first edition of this work was a reprint of a somewhat hastily written paper on change of air in the treatment of pulmonary consumption published in the Medical Mirror for 1864. Its circulation has been the means of bringing to the author's notice much interesting and striking evidence confirmatory of the truth of the views he has put forth; the main substance of these being to shew that what is called a bracing air is more constitutionally curative of pulmonary consumption, than one that is in a marked degree relaxing, and that the less lung a person has to breathe with, the more important is it that the air inhaled should be as bracing and tonic as can be borne if the nutrition of the body is to be duly maintained.

The observations of the great army surgeon Larrey, and others, quoted in these pages, will shew that these ideas are not new, and in these days when so much stress is laid on the tonic treatment of consumption it seems but reasonable to make a tonifying and invigorating climate assist the action of nutritious diet, cod-liver oil, and strengthening medicines.

Care has been taken to indicate, as clearly as possible, the sort of cases that may form exceptions to the above rule, and in which the palliative effects of a sedative climate are advisable.

Thus the author has endeavoured, in a spirit free from all undue prejudice, to prepare a work that may prove useful as a practical guide to the climatic treatment of chronic pulmonary affections, and it is in this character the work is to be regarded rather than as one professing to be completely descriptive of the various sanatory resorts mentioned.

Since some of the most cheering and satisfactory effects of change of climate are seen in increase of appetite and digestive power, it has been thought well to append to the second, as well as to the present edition, a short chapter on the diet and regimen of pulmonic invalids, especially as much has been added of late to our knowledge in these matters that is of practical utility.

PREFACE.

If some things in this chapter seem common-place truisms known to everybody, the excuse must be, that though known, and approved, they are still much neglected in the practical life of the invalid.

JOHN C. THOROWGOOD.

61 WELBECK STREET,
    CAVENDISH SQUARE.
        November 12th, 1868.

CONTENTS.

CHAPTER I.
                                                          PAGE

Introductory Remarks—Climates to be viewed in their effects on the system generally as well as on the lungs—Observations wanted on actual invalids in various climates—The experiment of twenty patients sent to winter at Madeira and its results 1

CHAPTER II.

Influence of climate in the cause and progress of Consumption or Phthisis—Pulmonary phthisis not a disease of cold climates—Relative mortality from phthisis in the Army and Navy—Beneficial effect of sea air—Rarity of consumption on the N.W. coast of Scotland—Elevation of districts—Climate of Mexico—Exposure to open air preventive of phthisis—The disease common in many warm places, as Italy and the West Indies—Damp air and soil most injurious—Effects of Marsh miasm—Practical rules 6

CHAPTER III.

Impurity of the Air and sedentary employment conducive to phthisis—Illustrations of the effects of a close atmosphere in causing lung disease—on the generally good effect of a pure and bracing air on consumptive persons 19

CHAPTER IV.

Of the cases of those who require a mild climate—Laryngeal phthisis and loss of voice—Mild climates good in the convalescence from inflammatory diseases of the lungs, such as pneumonia, bronchitis, croup, &c.—Places that possess a warm climate with more or less sedative character—Torquay and the South Devon coast—Places on the S. coast possessing a mild, yet tonic, air, Bournemouth; Stations in the Isle of Wight, Hastings, and St. Leonards—Sedative climates abroad, Madeira, Rome, Pisa, Pau—As a tonic climate, Arcachon—Causes of prevalent errors respecting the indiscriminate use of mild climates for the consumptive, illustrative case 26

CHAPTER V.

Dry and bracing climates—South of France—Nice, Cannes, Hyères—Illustration of good effects of air of Cannes—Sea air at Cannes apt to irritate—Mentone, St. Remo, Malaga, Upper Egypt and the Nile—Illustrative cases—Climates of Norway, Canada and Australia 44

CHAPTER VI.

On the more bracing climates of Great Britain—Causes of the variable nature of English climates—West coast of Scotland—Examples shewing the curative effects of the bracing air of the east coast of England in cases of confirmed phthisis—Signs of convalescence indicated by the cough—Places on the coast possessing a tonic and bracing air—Scarborough, Yarmouth, Cromer, Margate, Folkestone, Weymouth, The Channel Islands—Bracing climates found inland—Harrogate, Malvern, Buxton, Clifton, &c 57

CHAPTER VII.

Illustrations of the curative effect of a bracing air in advanced pulmonary disease—Opinions of numerous physicians and others confirming the author's views on this point—Curative effect of an open air life for those in advanced consumption—Practical conclusions and suggestions 67

CHAPTER VIII.

On the Diet and Digestion of pulmonary patients—Importance of exercise to ensure proper assimilation of Nutriment—Various kinds of food and drink—Preparations of Iceland Moss—Use of Whey—Diet under special circumstances—Of habits of life, exercise, sleep, Turkish bath, and cold bathing—Peculiar feeling of weakness, not always a bad sign—Concluding remarks 75

ON
CHANGE OF AIR
IN THE PREVENTION AND CURE
OF
CONSUMPTION AND OTHER CHRONIC LUNG DISEASES.

ERRATA.

Page 36. Line 5 from bottom for "*irratable*" read "*irritable*."
—— 38. Note marked † *refers to page* 40 *line* 8.
—— 71. Line 9 for "*is*" read "*as*."
—— 97. Line 17 for "*patient*" read "*patients*."

The physician, when called to a case of acute bronchitis or pneumonia, usually makes his first directions for treatment emphatically to bear on the regulation of the temperature of the patient's chamber, and means are at once taken to ensure free ventilation consistently with the maintenance of a due degree of warmth, and such an amount of moisture in the air as any special exigencies of the case may seem to demand.

ing a mild, yet tonic, air, Bournemouth; Stations in the Isle of Wight, Hastings, and St. Leonards—Sedative climates abroad, Madeira, Rome, Pisa, Pau—As a tonic climate, Arcachon—Causes of prevalent errors respecting the indiscriminate use of mild climates for the consumptive, illustrative case 26

CHAPTER V.

Dry and bracing climates—South of France—Nice, Cannes, Hyères—Illustration of good effects of air of Cannes—Sea air at Cannes apt to irritate—Mentone, St. Remo, Malaga, Upper Egypt and the Nile—Illustrative cases—Climates of Norway, Canada and Australia 44

others confirming the author's views on this point—Curative effect of an open air life for those in advanced consumption—Practical conclusions and suggestions 67

CHAPTER VIII.

On the Diet and Digestion of pulmonary patients—Importance of exercise to ensure proper assimilation of Nutriment—Various kinds of food and drink—Preparations of Iceland Moss—Use of Whey—Diet under special circumstances—Of habits of life, exercise, sleep, Turkish bath, and cold bathing—Peculiar feeling of weakness, not always a bad sign—Concluding remarks 75

ON
CHANGE OF AIR
IN THE PREVENTION AND CURE
OF
CONSUMPTION AND OTHER CHRONIC LUNG DISEASES.

CHAPTER I.

Introductory Remarks—Climates to be viewed in their effects on the system generally as well as on the lungs—Observations wanted on actual invalids in various climates—The experiment of twenty patients sent to winter at Madeira and its results.

In all affections, whether acute or chronic, of the lungs and air-passages, attention to the state of the atmosphere which surrounds the patient, and is therefore in constant and intimate contact with the diseased surfaces, is a matter of the very first importance.

The physician, when called to a case of acute bronchitis or pneumonia, usually makes his first directions for treatment emphatically to bear on the regulation of the temperature of the patient's chamber, and means are at once taken to ensure free ventilation consistently with the maintenance of a due degree of warmth, and such an amount of moisture in the air as any special exigencies of the case may seem to demand.

In the more chronic pulmonary affections, as phthisis, asthma, emphysema, and chronic bronchitis, the selection of an air and climate suitable for the invalid to reside in, is always a matter of anxious consideration. How can we reasonably expect to see a case of active phthisis, with great irritability and spasm of the air tubes, and frequent intercurrent inflammations, improve, while the patient is hourly drawing through his intensely susceptible chest a keen and cold, though doubtless highly bracing air; and, on the other hand how often do we see disastrous results follow on the removal of a patient, languid, exhausted, and perhaps far gone in actual pulmonic softening, to one of those humid, hot and enervating climates once held in high repute for the cure of pulmonary consumption of every kind and in every degree.

The object of the following pages will be to offer to the reader a few remarks on change of air as a means of preventing, alleviating, and curing pulmonary affections, and to afford aid in forming a judgment from recorded observations and experience as to what appear to be the best conditions of climate to cure or mitigate these diseases in their various forms and stages.

While we consider the atmosphere as a body in constant and intimate contact with the mucous membrane lining the air tubes and cells of the lungs, we must not forget that it is in equally intimate relation also to the skin covering the exterior of the body, and by its temperature, moisture, and degree of pressure, the air influences the functions of the skin, and the digestive and secretory organs in common with those of the aerian mucous membrane, or internal skin, which lines the air passages and lungs.

Hence it becomes necessary in the treatment of all chronic pulmonary diseases, to regard the effect of the climate that is resorted to on the general system, as well as on the lungs of the invalid, and be the temperature ever so uniform and warm, the rainy days few and far between, and the authorities who recommend the resort most eminent, a patient may be quite sure that if, after a few weeks spent in a place, he finds his appetite failing, his liver requiring to be stirred into action by the stimulus of mercury, and his inclination for exertion to be diminishing, he has made a great and injurious mistake and had better at once quit a climate which will clearly do him nothing but mischief.

That very pernicious blunders are constantly made by patients in their choice of a climate is a point very well known by those who have mixed among invalids in their climatic resorts. I believe the way to obviate, to some extent, these mishaps is to observe the actual invalid more closely, and not to be guided so entirely by tables of temperature, amount of rainfall, direction of winds and so forth; no work on climate seems to be thought in any way complete unless it abounds with a mass of carefully-recorded meteorological observations, and these in the form of lengthy tables occupy space some of which, at any rate, had better have been given to observations on the functions of the lungs, livers, and stomachs of the various kinds of invalids who were submitted to the action of the climate.

The kind of climatic experience we want is just such as was made in the most complete way possible by the Brompton Hospital when, in the years 1865-66, twenty well developed cases of consumption, carefully selected by most able authorities were sent to winter at Madeira. The report published on the return of these patients said that two out of the twenty returned improved, seven were slightly improved, twelve were no better and no worse, five were made worse, and one died. Such is the result of an experiment which is hardly likely to be repeated as far as Madeira is concerned though that beautiful island will still maintain its name for a warm mild climate, with an equable temperature, and will well enough suit those invalids who really require this description of climate and whose cases will be adverted to, further on in this work.

I have quoted this instance of the Madeira experiment, just to shew the direction in which our researches upon the curative powers of different climates ought to lead us; and although this experiment was not very satisfactory, as far as the patients were concerned, yet we have learnt much from it, and all owe their gratitude to those who devised and effected it.

In proceeding now to treat of those chronic pulmonary affections for the cure or palliation of which change of air is most commonly required, we will first take Consumption, or pulmonary phthisis, and see under what atmospheric conditions this disease is most apt to arise and progress, and what are the conditions of climate most likely to arrest it in its various stages, or to mitigate in some degree its injurious effects.

Pulmonary consumption being a disease so commonly engendered by an impure and unhealthy atmosphere, it will be well to devote some exclusive attention to the causation of this disease. Subsequently in speaking of the treatment of consumption by special climates, opportunity will be afforded to allude to other forms of chronic lung disease and their climatic requirements, for by so doing needless repetition will be avoided.

CHAPTER II.

Influence of climate in the cause and progress of Consumption or Phthisis—Pulmonary phthisis not a disease of cold climates—Relative mortality from phthisis in the Army and Navy—Beneficial effect of sea air—Rarity of consumption on the N.W. coast of Scotland—Elevation of districts—Climate of Mexico—Exposure to open air preventive of phthisis—The disease common in many warm places, as Italy and the West Indies—Damp air and soil most injurious—Effects of Marsh miasm—Practical rules.

ENQUIRING, in the first place, as to the sort of climate and atmosphere in which pulmonary consumption, or phthisis, is most apt to arise and make progress, we shall find good evidence to shew that this disease is by no means one peculiar to cold regions; for while in some of the cold and most exposed parts of the globe the disease is almost unknown, there are regions well known to be sheltered and warm, where phthisis is very frequent in its onset, and rapid and relentless in its progress.

The following observations, by various authorities, will tend to shew how free some of the cold regions of the North are from the prevalence of phthisis, and also how this disease appears to decrease in frequency with increase in the elevation of a district above the level of the sea.

In an interesting work by M. Boudin, chief surgeon of one of the military hospitals in Paris, we learn that there are countries where phthisis is quite unknown, as for instance, Iceland; no phthisical patients are seen in Finmark; and the Swedish physicians affirm that consumption becomes less common as we proceed northward; there is, in fact, such a thing as a preventing action in the Polar regions.

In England, army statistics show that the English soldier is more often a prey to phthisis in his own country than in any other. In the United Kingdom, the Infantry of the Line lose annually by phthisis 8·9 men per 1,000, and the Guards 12·5. At Malta, the mortality is below 5 per 1,000; at Gibraltar, the Mauritius, and Ceylon, 4; at the Cape, 3; and in the Madras Presidency, 1.*

In the navy the general mortality from phthisis is much lower than in the army, being on an average, for all the various stations, about 2·3 as the ratio per 1000 of mean force.

The constant inhalation of the fresh sea air, together with the manual labour constantly required of seamen, are doubtless powerful causes in diminishing the frequency of pulmonary consumption among this class of the community.

An eminent hospital physician, and author of "Clinical Lectures," once told me that were he to be afflicted with signs of incipient phthisis he should seek a cure in a prolonged cruise on the sea in a yacht. I have myself heard of an instance where a voyage to the Arctic regions in a whale ship proved in the highest

---

* The Lancet for 1857, page 90.

degree beneficial; fresh sea air of a most bracing and tonifying kind being continually inhaled, while at the same time the style of living on board was most free and sumptuous; and it is not difficult to understand how, in a patient whose vitality was getting low, and yet who had spirit enough for a whaling expedition, the failing nutrient powers might be wonderfully restored by such decidedly tonic treatment, and the signs of threatening consumption averted.

The great observer Laennec, was of opinion that sea air was antagonistic to the development of phthisis, and more recently this opinion has been confirmed by the observations of Dr. Verhægle* of Ostend who shews that while in the deaths in the interior of the country there are 19 per cent from phthisis, in the hospital at the sea port of Ostend there are but 6·60 as the per centage from the same cause. That sea air may, in certain states of lung, prove irritating, is a point to be alluded to and illustrated hereafter, when treating more specially of marine climates.

With respect to the civil community of Great Britain, it may be observed that among the deaths in London those from phthisis are 18 per cent; in Edinburgh 11·9; Leith 10·3; and Aberdeen 6·2.†

Further northward still the disease seems remarkably uncommon, for Mr. Keith Johnston, writing in

---

* See Syd. Soc. Year Book 1859, p. 222.
† The Lancet for 1857, page 90.

the Med: Chir: Review for 1857, observes; "that the opinion long entertained, that phthisis is a disease peculiar to cold climates is quite erroneous, for the disease is almost unknown in the Arctic regions, Siberia, the Orkneys, Shetlands, and Hebrides." The almost complete exception of the Faro Isles from consumption is specially noticed also by Dr. W. P. Alison in the Edinburgh Medical Journal for November 1855, and Dr. J. E. Morgan in the Brit. and For. Med. Chir. Rev., 1860, draws attention to the rarity of phthisis along the N. W. coast of Scotland, as established by his own observations and that of others.

In alluding to the possible causes of this immunity Dr. Morgan considers the most efficient of these to be the way in which the Highland cabins are constructed and the fact of their being warmed by means of peat-fires, the inhalation of the peat smoke seeming in a marked way to prevent and check the development of pulmonary tuberculosis.

In Oban where coal is chiefly used as a fuel, phthisis is by no means uncommon.

Fuchs shows, from extensive data, that in Northern Europe phthisis is most prevalent at the level of the sea, and that it decreases with increase of elevation to a certain point. At Marseilles, on the seaboard, the mortality from this disease is 25 per cent.; at Oldenburgh, eighty feet above the level of the sea, it is 30 per cent.; at Hamburgh forty eight feet above the sea it is 23 per cent.: while at Eschevege, four hundred and ninety-six feet above the sea level, it is only 12 per cent.; and at Brotterode, eighteen hundred feet above sea, it is but 0·9 per cent. It is calculated that in the temperate zone at least one-tenth of the population die of phthisis, and it is uniformly more fatal in cities than in the country. In England, the excess in cities is equal to 25 per cent.

Dr. Gastaldi is another observer who bears witness to the preventive and curative influence of mountain air over pulmonary phthisis, and Dr. Mühry a German writer on climates, seasons, and elevations, lays great stress on the respiration of the air of elevated districts as a means of promoting that free and complete expansion of the air cells of the lungs, which is such a very important desideratum for the prevention of phthisis. The effect of breathing the rarified air of highly elevated districts is to cause great expansion of the chest in consequence of the large volume of air required for the purposes of respiration. In a recent article on the climate of the table land of Mexico, lying from 3000 to 8000 feet above the level of the sea, the air of this upland district is spoken of as being very trying to those not accustomed to it, while the natives, and those able to bear a process of acclimatization to this atmosphere, are remarkable for the immense development of chest which they acquire in consequence of the necessity there is for breathing a large volume of rarified air in order to obtain enough oxygen for the requirements of the system.

In Mexico one travels for miles at the height of Mont Cenis, the St. Gothard, or the Gt. St. Bernard enjoying an air which Englishmen and Frenchmen call mild, though the Spaniards are inclined to think it keen and cold, and for those in whose lungs there is active disease, all allow that this air is too sharp and exciting.

We can understand from these remarks, the use of the climate of a very elevated district, to cause free development and expansion of the lungs, but where disease is in active progress, and where actual inflammation is present, it is easy to see how this expansive process may increase irritation and so add to the danger and mischief; hence we should infer that these very lofty regions are better adapted to prevent the development of threatening pulmonary disease, by causing free expansion of the chest, than to cure it when it is in active and acute progress.

In the American Journal of Medical Science, Dr. Flint has furnished the details of 24 examples of arrest of phthisis that have occurred in his own practice, and added interesting observations upon the circumstances which seemed to favour such arrest. In five cases in which the disease was thus arrested the sole treatment consisted in causing the individuals to abandon sedentary occupations for those entailing abundant out-door exercise; and eight others, in whose cases the disease after a time spontaneously came to a stand still, were persons of active out-door habits.

"The exercise in open air" (says Dr. Flint) was not generally of the kind which often goes by that title, consisting in simple airings by gentle walks or drives; but it consisted in rough occupation, involving at times great exposure to vicissitudes of weather."

Change of climate occurred only in two cases prior to evidence of arrest. On this subject of climate Dr. Flint has been led to believe (with many others) that "climate in itself exerts no special agency in determining an arrest of the disease, but that it may favour this result indirectly by affording better opportunity for exercise in the open air, and furnishing objects of interest to the mind which will secure that object."

The above quoted remarks, from such a careful and experienced observer, are most important; experience from the time of Sydenham has been continually showing how out door exercise, especially when taken on horse back, can break through a constitutional tendency to consumption, and can even aid most powerfully to arrest the disease when it is fairly in progress. Sydenham used to say that horse exercise was as much a specific for incipient consumption, as was bark for the ague, and the late Dr. Parrish of Philadelphia believed that he cured himself of consumption by travelling on his rounds in a vehicle without springs, using this as a substitute for a saddle itself.

We see now from the foregoing observations collected from various trust-worthy, and competent authorities, that pulmonary phthisis, is a comparatively rare disease in Northern regions, where the air is pretty uniformly cold and bracing, and rare also in those regions which are situate at considerable elevation above the level of the sea; nor is the disease often met with among those persons whose occupations cause them to spend much time employed in the open air.

It remains next to examine into the prevalence of phthisis in the warmer quarters of the globe, and then to take a glance at those social conditions of life most conducive of this same disease.

Dr. Pollock, in his lectures in the Lancet for 1856, speaking of climate and its relation to phthisis, says, that there is no region of the earth absolutely free from this disease. "In the West Indian Islands it is met with in its most severe and rapid form, and in Italy, the country to which so many consumptive invalids are exported, it is a disease of universal prevalence and great intensity," as Dr. Pollock has himself witnessed, "so that the Italians regard the disease as contagious and malignant."

It is shown in some tables given by Dr. Fuller in his work on the lungs, that in the civil hospitals of Rome and Naples 1 in 3·4 and 1 in 2·33 of the deaths from all causes are due to phthisis; while in Paris the proportion is 1 in 5·5. In London 1 in 6·2 and in Philadelphia 1 in 7·7.

We must remember here however that the habits of the people are not the most conducive to the cure of pulmonary disease, bad ventilation within doors, poor diet, and want of attention to cleanliness of the skin, doubtless contribute to hasten the progress of phthisis when once developed.

Among the Swiss, it has been noticed by Dr. H. Weber, that phthisis is not often found among the men who are continually out of doors among the mountains, but among the women who keep indoors and do not get much air and exercise, the disease is very frequent.

So, again, Dr. Livingstone, the African explorer, has shown that the native tribes of South Africa, who live entirely an out of doors life, and know nothing of town employments, are free from consumption.

The great prevalence of phthisis in the West, as opposed to the East Indies, has been noticed by Staff Surgeon Hunter in the Med: Times and Gazette for 1850. In the East Indies where the climate is dry, the disease is almost at its minimum, and Dr. Hunter especially recommends, Poona, in the Bombay Presidency, also Madras and Bangalore as places healthy as England in most respects, and eminently adapted for the generality of phthisical invalids. Of Bombay; and the Malabar coast, generally, he speaks less favourably.

We have now seen that phthisis may be very rare in the cold and elevated part of the globe, and very common in some of those regions which are warm and sheltered, but of all the climates to induce the disease, none can equal one that is at once damp and cold.

The temperature and pressure of an atmosphere loaded with watery vapour will be liable to considerable variations, since aqueous vapour is the chief fluctuating ingredient in the air, and hence is by no means a safe atmosphere for the consumptive or bronchitic invalid.

Increase of the amount of watery vapour in the atmosphere generally produces a fall in the Barometer, hence in extra-tropical regions, such a fall in the mercury, without a change or rise in the wind, is usually followed by rain as a result of this increase of moisture.

The first effect however of the increase of moisture in the air, and of the fall of the Barometer, is diminished pressure, so that it is reckoned, supposing the atmospheric pressure on a man of ordinary stature to be 30,000 lbs. that a fall of half an inch in the column of mercury in the Barometer is equivalent to a reduction of 500 lbs. pressure on the body.

In consequence of this diminished pressure the vessels become engorged and secretion determined, and yet this does not take place inasmuch as the air is already saturated with watery vapour, hence arises a feeling of languor, fatigue, and sweating on the least exertion, and in cases of bronchitis with profuse secretion the patient's danger is of necessity increased by this diminished pressure and coincident augmentation of humidity in the air.

Dr. Africanus Horton, in his recently published work on the climate of Western Africa, observes, that dry heat was infinitely less productive of disease than heat combined with humidity.

Dr. Horton (p. 209,) noticed that at McCarthy's Island, and in the countries interior of the Gambia region, the month of October was the most unhealthy of the season, the atmosphere being hot and moist, and dysentery, diarrhœa, and virulent fever, very prevalent. When the hot dry winds blow disease falls to its minimum, and the months of February, March, and April, although the hottest of the year, are the most healthy.

Many years ago it was observed by Sir J. Clark that "of all the physical qualities of the air, humidity is the most injurious to animal life," and the French observer Fourcault considers dampness in the air to be the great cause of consumption and intermittent fevers.

The objectionable character of a marshy district is well known, and is in great measure due to the damp emanations which arise from these regions. M. Pallas, of the French army in Algeria, considers that marshes affect much the electricity of the air. I quote his observations for they are very important.

1. As light and air are the essential agents of vision and respiration, so electricity is the functional agent of enervation.

2. The greater number of diseases, and especially those of the nervous class, are occasioned by the exaggerated influence of general electricity, of which clouds, storms, and marshy regions are the most fruitful sources.

3. Marshes in their geological constitution, and in the effects which they produce upon the economy, present the greatest analogy to the galvanic pile. Thus their action is much the more baneful, as they

contain certain proportions of water, and their activity is considerably increased when the water contains organic or saline matter in a state of solution. This explains why salt marshes, and such as are near maritime rivers are the most insalubrious. The drying up or submersion of marshes produces analogous conditions to those of a galvanic pile deprived of humidity, or which is under water, and the effects of which are then insignificant.

The researches of philosophers and physiologists have shewn that the electricity produced by our machines exerts a special action upon the nervous system. Experience and observations of facts, prove that the diseases which are produced by marshy atmospheres are primarily nervous, and become inflammatory only by the reaction of the nerves upon the vascular system, inducing consecutive local or general irritation. (See Horton on *Climate of W. Africa.*)

These considerations in reference to the consumptive are worthy of much attention. My own belief is, and always has been, that the nervous system is intimately involved in pulmonary tuberculosis, and if we wish to cure the diseased tendency in the system it is certain that any cause of nervous depression or exhaustion must be most carefully shunned. We further see, as one practical rule to be deduced from the foregoing observations, that those disposed to all forms of tubercular disease will do well to follow, is to endeavour to have a residence on a dry soil, and at a moderate elevation where there will be free circulation of air, and to avoid places lying low where the air is damp, stagnant, and cold.

The fact that a damp and retentive soil is a very powerful inducer of consumption in those resident thereupon has been most incontrovertibly shewn by Dr. Buchanan in his interesting report in the tenth volume of the Health Report of the Privy Council.

We now proceed to notice the social relations of of life under which lung disease is prone to arise and advance.

CHAPTER III.

Impurity of the Air and sedentary employment conducive to phthisis—Illustrations of the effects of a close atmosphere in causing lung disease—on the generally good effect of a pure and bracing air on consumptive persons.

The report of the deaths in England and Wales, by the Registrar General for one year, gives about twelve out of every hundred deaths to pulmonary consumption as the general rate, but in cities, as has been already stated, this per centage is very much higher.

A glance at some of the following figures will shew the relative mortality from phthisis in town and country.*

In Hertfordshire the mortality from consumption is 179 in 100,000 annually; it is 363 in 100,000 in Liverpool; 331 in 100,000 in Manchester; 277 in 100,000 in London; 100 in 100,000 in Norway.

The causes of this excess of mortality in the large towns is to be found in the sedentary employment of the inhabitants, and the close and impure air which of necessity they are compelled continually to breathe. Thus Dr. E. Smith, in his 6th Report on the sanitary state of tailors in London, notices consumption and

* From remarks on phthisis by Dr. Drysdale, in Medical Mirror, March, 1865.

other chest affections as the most common cause of death among them. In illustration of the tendency of a close and confined atmosphere to produce pulmonary consumption the following table compiled by Dr. Guy, will be of interest. The table is based upon measurements of the offices of letterpress printers, and the number of compositors working in them, together with the answers of certain simple questions addressed to the men themselves.

	Number per cent Spitting blood.	Subject to Catarrh.
104 men having less than 500 cubic feet of air to breathe.	12·50.	12·50.
115 men having from 500 to 600 cubic feet of air.	4·35.	3·48.
101 men having more than 600 cubic feet of air.	3·96.	1·98.

Of 652 cases of undoubted phthisis observed by Dr. Pollock, 393, more than half, were individuals following sedentary in-door employments, conditions which, as Dr. Pollock observes, imply two things which are preeminently conducive to phthisis—want of fresh air, and a minimum of muscular waste and renewal. In those of the consumptive poor who, whether from choice or by necessity, confine themselves entirely to one small close room, the progress of their disease is truly fearful to witness, and our most approved remedies absolutely worthless.

With respect to the influence of the air of crowded cities, I have noticed very often during eight years in hospital and dispensary practice how, among the poorer classes, phthisis has commenced its attack soon after the individual, previously resident in the country, had settled in some of the densely populated regions of London; and I have been struck in numerous instances with the marked improvement which has taken place on the patient quitting town to go for a season into a country district, reputed even somewhat unhealthy, but where the air would be purer and fresher than it could be in the courts and alleys of London.

When the remove has been to a healthy part of the country, the improvement has been proportionably much greater.

In the case of some, who from living in a close atmosphere have got into a low state of vitality, I have noticed a tendency to congestion of the upper third of one or both lungs; a very incipient stage of tubercular disease perhaps, that is surely and speedily removed by tonics and pure air.

In the Report of the health of the Royal Navy, for the year 1860, are to be found some most interesting accounts of a form of congestive pneumonia of the lung apex which had much the character of incipient phthisis, and was, in the opinion of the Surgeons, caused partly by unavoidable over-crowding of the men in their berths between the decks.

The surgeon of the St Jean d'Acre, in his nosological synopsis, returned 117 cases of this "Cachexia Pulmonalis" and 102 of Phthisis. The total number of cases of disease referable to the pulmonary organs noted from April, when the vessel was at Malta, up to the end of the year, amounted to 285 ; of these 112 were invalided, and 6 terminated in death.

Searching into the cause of this large amount of pulmonary disease the surgeon (Dr. Edmonds) drew attention to the crowded state of the lower deck, where about 930 men slept, the hammock hooks being only 14 inches apart; thus a compact mass of human beings extended along the deck, and it was noticed in April that there was a difference of from 8° to 12° in the temperature of the air below and above the hammocks.

By improving the state of the ventilation and clearing out decaying matters that had collected in the ships bottom, the health of the crew by degrees improved, and the surgeon remarks (page 81 of the report) that although the symptoms, both general and physical, were all suggestive of phthisis in its early stage, yet a great number of those who were invalided, rapidly improved when they arrived in England, and soon afterwards were able to rejoin the service.

The whole of the above quoted report is well worth careful study, for it shows just what are the conditions likely to develop very serious and troublesome disease in the lungs and air passages, and also what appear the best means of prevention and cure.

With respect to elevation of a district as a means of insuring a pure air, I may say that I have had frequent opportunity of observing the great prevalence and rapid progress of phthisis in many country villages lying low and damp, as compared with others which are placed higher, and where consequently the air is not so stagnant and humid.

In some of the districts with which I am familiar, lying north of London, and said to be about on a level with the cross on the top of St. Paul's, phthisis is a rare disease when compared with its prevalence in those parts of the north-eastern, eastern, and southern districts, where the level is very much lower.*

More than one instance of striking and lasting improvement in cases of unmistakable phthisis has come under my notice in the case of persons who have removed from low-lying country districts to the more elevated situations.

When we consider that pulmonary consumption is in the majority of cases a disease of debility, and specially, as I believe, in its earliest stages, of debility and exhaustion of the nervous force, we can quite understand the benefit likely to accrue to the patient from dwelling in a pure fresh air which increases the appetite and powers of digestion, stimulates the free and perfect expansion of the lungs, and thus promotes the formation of healthy blood and the nutrition of the whole system.

Moreover under such physiological conditions of existence, medical treatment by cod-liver oil, chalybeates, and other tonics, will have far greater efficacy than it would have under other circumstances; inas-

---

* Since writing the above I have observed some statistics collected by Dr Crisp. He finds that while at Chelsea 1 person in 28 died of consumption, at Hampstead only 1 in 61 died of the same disease.—*Med. Times*, Sept. 5th, 1868.

much as in a dry bracing air these remedies will be readily digested and assimilated by the system, while in a relaxing warm atmosphere they nauseate the stomach, disorder the liver and often have to be laid aside entirely.

While thus recommending the bracing air of elevated districts as a very important item in that general tonic treatment which experience is daily showing to be the best method of counteracting the tendency to tubercular disease, it must not be understood that every kind and degree of pulmonary phthisis is to be cured by bracing air, any more than by any regular routine of tonic medicine. In some forms of phthisis iron is a priceless remedy; while in others I have seen it prove most injurious, and so that dry bracing air, which is the best of tonics for very many, indeed for the generality, of cases of phthisis, is absolutely intolerable to others differently constituted or in a different stage of the malady—a matter which I now proceed to consider and illustrate more in detail.

We must always bear in mind, in dealing with such a disease as pulmonary phthisis, that we have in the first place to overcome a morbid constitutional tendency in the system; and, secondly we have to combat with symptoms of local disease as manifested in the lungs.

The attainment of the first of the objects above named should be the aim of a rational system of medicine; and provided the actual destruction of lung substance be not great, the probability is, that in the treatment best adapted to remedy the constitutional vice, we find the best palliatives for actual chest symptoms themselves.

The various preparations of iron, or some of the mineral acids, will often speedily cure a cough, which has been daily getting worse in proportion as the stomach has been drugged, truly *ad nauseam*, with ipecacuanha, squills, paregoric, and all the whole genus of expectorants.

Expectorants and sedatives are useful, indeed invaluable, at times, as adjuvants, in combating special symptoms, but growing experience shows that it is to the plan of tonic and invigorating constitutional treatment that we must look as the great method for the prevention and cure of phthisis in far the majority of cases.

CHAPTER. IV.

Of the cases of those who require a mild climate—Laryngeal phthisis and loss of voice—Mild climates good in the convalescence from inflamatory diseases of the lungs, such as pneumonia, bronchitis, croup, &c—Places that possess a warm climate with more or less sedative character—Torquay and the South Devon coast—Places on the S. coast possessing a mild yet tonic air, Bournemouth, stations in the Isle of Wight, Hastings and St Leonards—Sedative climates abroad, Madeira, Rome, Pisa, Pau. As a tonic climate, Arcachon—Causes of prevalent errors respecting the indiscriminate use of mild climates for the consumptive, illustrative case.

BEFORE proceeding to treat of the curative powers of a dry and bracing atmosphere in cases of pulmonary consumption it will be well to advert to those cases where a mild and sedative climate is indicated, and to mention some of the places where such a climate can be obtained in the greatest perfection; for just as we find in our medicinal treatment of consumption that there are times and seasons in the course of the disease during which the local symptoms of bronchitic irritation are so predominant as to oblige us to lay aside tonics, and use, for a time, some of the various sedative and expectorant remedies; so we find in the treatment of the disease by climate certain cases, and certain periods of the complaint, requiring the soothing influence of a mild air, and in noticing some of the health resorts for the phthisical in England and abroad, I purpose first to notice those climates which are warm and sedative and the use they have in the treatment of pulmonary disease. Examples of this kind of climate are to be found at Torquay, Penzance, Rome, Pisa, Pau, Madeira, and the Azores; places spoken of by Dr. Walshe, in the appendix to the second edition of his Treatise on the Diseases of the Heart and Lungs, as " possessing in varying degree a soft relaxing air, moderately high thermometric range, and most suitable to pulmonary and cardiac affections attended with irritability of the skin and mucous membranes and little disposition to general constitutional languor."

This tendency to general irritability of the system, with great proneness to intercurrent attacks of inflammation on the air-passages, and at the same time fair action of the stomach, liver, and bowels generally marks the class of patients for whom a mild and warm climate is suitable.

Those who have much languor of system, profuse sweating, excessive expectoration, tendency to biliousness, to hepatic congestion, or to diarrhœa and dysentery, will get nothing but harm from a warm sedative climate and therefore must by all means avoid it.

My own experience leads me to speak favourably of the mild climates for cases of true laryngeal phthisis in its early stages, where there is much hoarseness, or even complete extinction of the voice, with intense susceptibility of the throat to the slightest change of temperature. I have seen great benefit accrue in these cases from a residence in the

South of England at such places as Torquay, and more especially at Bournemouth. We all know how a patient of this class always comes to us carefully muffled up with a respirator, and it certainly is better that the patient should wear one of these instruments than that the throat should be exposed to cold wind or night air; when however we have placed the patient in a suitable climate then the sooner the respirator can be abandoned the better if a real and permanent cure be the object aimed at.

Another set of patients for whom a moderately warm air is essential are those who are convalescent from some acute pulmonary disorder, such as bronchitis or pneumonia. After the former of these complaints there often remains a rather obstinate cough, with difficulty of breathing and want of strength, so that the patient and his friends begin to think Asthma, or what appears worse, Consumption, is surely impending: So too after an attack of pneumonia, I have known very evident consolidation of lung persist for months, naturally giving just cause for anxiety, and yet this, just as the above detailed sequelæ of bronchitis, will vanish in the most satisfactory way possible under the influence of a mild, warm, and pure atmosphere. I can recall several cases that have been under my observation, both among outpatients at Victoria Park Hospital and elsewhere, where the patients have sought advice in consequence of symptoms such as those above detailed in which a short residence at Hastings has afforded striking relief to all the morbid symptoms.

In the cases of very young children, subject to, or convalescent from, attacks of true inflammatory croup, a mild and warm air is, as a general rule, highly beneficial; for it is important, in order to ensure a permanent cure in these instances, that the little patient should be exercised freely in the open air, and it will be found a matter of necessity, at least till every sign of inflammatory tendency has ceased, that this air should be mild and uniform in its temperature. Tenby in S. Wales, Bournemouth, the Isle of Wight, and St. Leonards, are all places likely to agree well in such instances, being mild and yet not unduly relaxing.

On the subsidence of all inflammatory symptoms, should there be languor of the system and nervous excitability, then a more bracing climate will be required, more especially if there be any symptom of Laryngismus Stridulus, or "child crowing," for this is a purely nervous affection, due to spasmodic closure of the larynx, and one which a cold and bracing air will often do more towards curing than any other method of medication, a point brought prominently before the profession by Mr. Roberton of Manchester.* Bracing places like Margate, Brighton, Malvern, Harrogate, and the Yorkshire coast are the parts of England then to be thought of for the invalid.

We now proceed briefly to describe some of those mild and sedative climates which are to be found in the South West of England, at such places as Tor-

---

* See Medical Times and Gazette, Jan. 14, 1865.

quay, Sidmouth, Penzance and other districts not far distant.

The general winter temperature of this S. W. coast is about two degrees higher than that of the coast of Sussex and Hampshire, and from three to four degrees higher than that of London. The atmosphere generally is soft, more or less humid and relaxing, very good during the coldest months of the winter for those in whom symptoms of general feverish irritation predominate with harshness and dryness of the skin, irritative or sub-inflammatory dyspepsia, and tendency to laryngeal disease, loss of voice, dry tight cough, and painful difficulty of breathing in the slighest cold.

Torquay is drier than many parts of this coast, free from fog, with a calm and equable air, and is well adapted as a winter residence for such cases as those that have been described and that require a mild sedative climate. In cases of advanced consumption, or of consumption complicated with disease of the liver, it is a climate productive of but little good and the best it can do is by its sedative properties to facilitate an easy and painless death. No greater mistake can be made than to send a patient with much languor of system, cavities in his lungs, and every sign of advanced consumption, to one of the mild climates of the South. It has been most truly said by Dr Fuller, at page 483 of his work on Diseases of the Lungs, that, "the rapid progress which con-"sumption sometimes makes in patients who have "gone abroad for their health, and which is often "attributed to their having delayed their journey too "long, is referable in most instances to the fact of "the individuals in question being persons who are "naturally benefited by a cool, bracing atmosphere, "and who sink at once when sent to the enervating "climate of the south."

To return however to the right use of the mild climates—

*Dr Shapter, of Exeter, gives as the result of his very extensive experience of the climates of the south-west coast, that it appears to act favourably in cases of great pulmonic irritability, sometimes found associated with the onset of tubercular disease of the lungs. In cases also of inflammatory or gastric dyspepsia, the climate usually suits well, especially if this form of dyspepsia be associated, as it frequently is, with a harsh, dry, inactive skin, for the warmth and humidity of the air tend to encourage that transudation from the skin which is the result of the vital action of the cutaneous surface itself. The relief also which the lungs experience when a dry skin is induced to moderate action is great, for matters are thus safely eliminated from the system which would otherwise be deposited on the lungs to form tubercles.

Rullmann, in "The Dublin Journal of Medicine," for 1861, considers that the mild climatic sanatoria of southern districts are useful as winter residences in the chronic bronchial catarrh and chronic tuberculosis of patients from more northern districts. Sum-

* Dublin Med. Quarterly, 1863, p. 441.

mer in these regions is often most injurious by developing and aggravating pulmonary mischief.

The same writer goes on to say, that the cases best suited by a moist and warm climate are attended by a very sensitive condition of the bronchial mucous membrane, frequent cough, dry, or possibly attended with viscid expectoration, and an excitable state of the vascular and nervous systems.

I agree entirely with these authorities as to the use to be made of a mild relaxing climate in the treatment of pulmonary affections.

It is not needful for me specially to describe the climates of Sidmouth, Dawlish, or Penzance; they are mild relaxing climates, and, as such, have their proper use in the treatment of pulmonary invalids. I should be disposed to place Torquay foremost on the list of the mild Sanatoria of the South West of England and where the indications, as already noted, are for a very mild and sedative winter climate, in which there will be but little risk of catching cold and so increasing laryngeal irritation and active chest disease, I do not think a better, or safer place, can be found than Torquay. The invalid can, if desirable, be close to the sea-shore, or can make his choice of various degrees of elevation around, and a moderate degree of elevation has seemed to me to suit best; the soil is dry, and yet the air is sufficiently humid to temper it to the requirements of an over-sensitive mucous membrane, and the patient who suffers much with irritation of the larynx, and loss of voice in the cold, and who has active sub-inflammatory phthisis going on in his chest, will be as safe to get through the winter comfortably as he well can be in an English climate.

Some invalids, for whom Torquay is too relaxing, find the climate of Tenby, South Wales, to agree well with them; for though the winter thermometric range at Tenby is high, yet the air is less relaxing and more tonic than it is at Torquay.

The South Coast of England, lying between Hastings and Portland Island, is an intermediate climate, being less warm, and far less relaxing than the South Devon Coast, and yet not so bracing as some of the places to be named presently.

On this part of the coast is Bournemouth, a well sheltered place, surrounded like Arcachon in France, with pine woods, the emanations from which, in warm weather, have a beneficial effect over diseased lungs.

As a general place of resort for persons affected with Asthma, Chronic Bronchitis, Phthisis in its earlier stages, Chronic Hoarseness and loss of voice, Bournemouth is certainly an excellent place. I cannot call to mind a single instance of a patient who has not found benefit from a residence there during the winter months.

The air is dry, warm, and tonic; owing to this dryness of the air and soil, the morning air is soon heated, so that, according to the observations of Mr. E. J. Sandars, the mean daily temperature is reached as early as 7.30 A.M. in the month of June, and it is therefore in the power of an invalid to have a long day out of doors, a matter of the very first importance, for if there be a specific for the cure of consumption it is a life in the open air.

Further east along this coast are other well-known places; among them the Isle of Wight presents a mild equable climate well adapted for the residence of pulmonary invalids during the year. From my own experience, and that of others, I can adduce instances of most striking improvement induced in patients threatened with phthisis by the pure tonifying air of this Island.

Ryde, and Cowes, on the north side of the Island, have seemed to me admirable summer quarters for the invalid, and during the winter, from November to the Spring, a change can be made to Undercliff and Ventnor, if the patient finds it too cold for him to be much out of doors on the North Coast of the Island.

Cases of bronchitic asthma I have found to be more comfortable, and make better progress, at these last-named places than at the part on the North about Ryde.

Hastings and St Leonards, though usually taken as one place, possess different climates, for while St Leonards may be placed among the tonic and moderately bracing climates, Hastings certainly belongs to the mild and sedative group. As has been already said, cases of irritable chest and windpipe, with tendency to inflammatory action, do well at Hastings; obstinate thickenings of the air tubes and consolidations of the lungs, I have observed to disappear satisfactorily during a residence there, a good result partly due doubtless to the highly marine character of the air. Cases of confirmed and and advanced phthisis with frequent haemoptysis I have seen made worse by the Hastings air, and these cases may with advantage move to St Leonards, if they desire to remain on the South Coast.

The climate of St Leonards may be called an intermediate one: the air is pure, fresh, and far more bracing than that of the Isle of Wight or Torquay; for a large number of cases of confirmed, and even advanced phthisis, I believe it to be a place deserving the good name it has acquired. The recent improvements in the town drainage by Mr Bazalgette, whereby the sea and beach are kept free from all impurities, will materially increase the salubrity of St Leonards. The highly marine character of the St Leonards air, in some instances, proves irritating to the larynx and to the air tubes, in other cases the saline impregnation of the air seems to prove decidedly curative.

St Leonards stands for the most part on the Tunbridge Wells sand; there is considerable range of elevation within the inhabited parts of the town, affecting of course the natural drainage. Most parts of the town are dry, and it appears from enquiries made by Dr. Greenhill, of Hastings, that if the deaths of visitors from consumption could be separated from the general return, then the mortality from indigenous phthisis would be found exceedingly small as compared with other places. For statistics of the relative prevalence of phthisis in Hastings, Tunbridge Wells, and other places in Kent, Surrey, and Sussex, I would refer the reader to Dr. Buchanan's excellent paper in the 10th Report of the Medical Officer of the Privy Council, p. 57—110.

It sometimes happens that an invalid, in whose case a mild air is indicated, prefers to seek this in some foreign land; either he has tried some of the mild climates of England with but partial satisfaction, or an entire change of scene and manner of living may be desirable. I mention here some of the foreign health resorts in which a mild and sedative climate can be found. First is the Island of Madeira.

Should a patient who presents symptoms of severe laryngeal and pulmonic irritation, be for leaving England altogether, he will do well to think of Madeira as likely to afford him a complete and salutary change.

Dr. Southey found that it was rare for the temperature of the coldest nights, in the part of Madeira close to the sea, to fall below 58°, and should this level prove too warm and relaxing, any degree of elevation above it can be obtained up even to a region of snow.

About Funchal the air of Madeira is humid and relaxing, but free from fog, and very soothing to irratable lungs, and it is rare that the rain fall prevents a daily opportunity for exercise on foot or on horseback; these matters, coupled with the sea voyage which the transit involves, form the recommendations of Madeira as a winter climate for that limited number of the phthisical who require a continuance of a mild, warm, and rather humid, climate.

Of other similar mild climates I believe Rome, and Pisa, to be two of the best and safest, I have known a patient unable to stand the bracing air of the coast of Provence, after spending a few months at Rome, till the signs of chest irritation were in a measure quieted, return again to the south of France and then derive great benefit from the air of Cannes and Hyères. Just as when, in our medicinal treatment of phthisis, by the temporary use of sedatives, we remove bronchitic irritation, and then build up the constitution by means of ferruginous tonics.

The climate of Pisa approaches somewhat to that of Madeira; it is more moist than Rome and is eminently soothing and antiphlogistic; in the dry bronchitis of old people, and in incipient phthisis with much bronchial irritation and spasm, it is for a season at any rate, a useful climate. Mr Matthews, in his "Diary of an Invalid" (a book in which some of the continental sanatoria, as Naples and Nice, are very strongly denounced) says, "I believe that Pisa is the very best place on the continent, during the winter, for complaints of the chest." I have recently had under my care, a young physician affected with signs of early phthisis with inflammatory tendency and frequent hæmoptysis; he passed a part of last winter at Pisa and found the air to suit him well for time. Another patient, also a medical man, complained to me of the dulness of the place, and of the cold wind that now and then came down from the mountains. In summer and autumn Pisa is to be avoided, and in the second stage of phthisis it is, like all relaxing places, most pernicious.

The mean annual temperature of Pisa is 59°;—winter 44°; Spring 57°; Summer 73°; and Autumn 62°

Another much frequented winter resort, to which it is estimated about *2000 English invalids, most of them consumptive, annually go, is Pau, and a few words on this place and its climate will not be out of place here.

Pau stands on a gravelly soil 700 feet above the sea, on a sort of terrace facing the Pyrenées, and is very completely protected from winds, hence, as Sir J. Clark observes, "calmness is the striking character of the climate." The mean annual temperature is four and a half degrees higher than that of London, and the average rain-fall at Pau is 40 inches, while in London it is 27. Notwithstanding this large fall of rain, the ground, from the nature of the soil, drys fast, and the air is not reckoned damp, for steel articles do not rust, and uninhabited houses never show any signs of damp.†

The climate of Pau is clear, free from fog, and equable, being, in this respect, superior to Rome and Pisa. Patients who suffer from tendency to inflammation, and great nervous irritation, and those in

---

* Dr Taylor on climate of Pau, 2nd edit., 1856.

† See Sir Dominic Corrigan's address to the College of Physicians of Ireland (1860-61).

an early stage of phthisis, with tendency to hæmoptysis with a dry irritable constitution, usually are the ones to get good from a winter at Pau. In diseases attended with an atonic relaxed state of system, it is a climate likely to act prejudicially. Those of an apoplectic, scrofulous, or lymphatic, temperament, do well to avoid Pau.

Dr. Madden, of Dublin, in a valuable book on Climate, published in 1864, as the result of large experience with carefully recorded observations, devotes a chapter to Pau, but is unable to bear testimony to the uniformity of its temperature, and with respect to humidity, as denoted by the hygrometer, Dr. Madden finds Pau to be about on a par with Kew near London. During November 1861, the mean moisture of the air by the hygrometer was 82° at Pau compared with 85° at Kew; and in December it was at Pau 83° and at Kew exactly the same.

Not very far from Pau, in a vast bay on the south west coast of France and accessible by railway, is situate Arcachon, a place fast rising into well-deserved repute as in every respect good for pulmonary invalids.

At Arcachon the air may be called tonic, with less marine impregnation than exists in the air of the neighbouring stations of Biarritz or Royau, where the sea is rougher and more agitated by wind. In summer the heat is rarely felt to be oppressive, and there are good opportunities of sea-bathing from June till the end of September.

During one very severe winter at Arcachon, Dr.

Hameau, the resident physician, found the thermometer only fell to freezing point four times in December and three times in February. With all the advantages of a good sea air, Arcachon is protected from severe gales by moderately high sand hills, and all around it are thick pine woods, the terebinthinate emanations from which impregnate the atmosphere and have a salutary effect over diseased lungs.

In England the nearest approach to such a climate as that of Arcachon will be found on the Hampshire coast at Bournemouth. Both places possessing a tonic, equable and moderately warm air, and therefore suited to the requirement of a large number of pulmonic invalids, whether bronchitic, phthisical or asthmatic.

With respect to the places I have mentioned as affording examples of a sedative and relaxing air, I would say that from what I have myself observed, and gathered from the observation of others, I believe the actual *curative* power of these relaxing climates, whether in England or abroad over confirmed pulmonary consumption has been greatly overrated; though sometimes, in certain early stages of the disease, where there is much susceptibility and bronchitic irritation about the chest, their effect may for a time be of great service. In many cases of asthma and dry chronic bronchitis the effect of these sedative climates is most strikingly beneficial and curative.

One reason why both in England and abroad so many of the relaxing climates have come to be regarded as good for consumption and even essential to the continued existence of all and every one afflicted with phthisis, in no matter what stage, is, that very often the local symptoms of pain, cough, etc. are much relieved by the inhalation of a warm moist air, and this mere mitigation of symptoms is regarded too exclusively, so that the patient is often retained in a relaxing climate till it begins to act most injuriously as a depressor of the general constitutional vigour. Then again, as has been already said, cases of asthma and chronic bronchitis get well often in a relaxing air, and these are apt to be set down as instances of genuine phthisis cured by climatic influence. The condition of the appetite and digestion I believe to be a more trustworthy guide and indicator of progress, than the mere chest symptoms alone.

The following case will illustrate how a too exclusive regard to the mere local chest symptoms, some years ago, led the writer of these pages into error, in advising a change of climate to an invalid. The patient was a gentleman of experience in climates, tall, thin, nervous and weak from long illness; he had lost a sister with phthisis, and after a rather sharp attack of pneumonia, decided symptoms of the same disease attacked him, and by the advice of Dr. Williams, he left this country to travel abroad; he spent the summer in Switzerland, having passed the previous winter at Rome and Pisa. I met him at Cannes in the south of France, whither he had come for the winter; he then had a small cavity at the upper part of one lung, a good deal of expectoration, and now and then a little blood tinged the sputa; the appetite and digestion were feeble, and there was a good deal of general debility. The result of this gentleman's experience of climate was to him disappointing and unsatisfactory; at Nice he suffered much from pain at the chest, blood spitting and difficulty of breathing, but, after staying at Cannes, he improved considerably, and could take and digest a fair amount of cod-liver oil.

Though improving in general health and strength, the lung symptoms did not show much amendment, and it seemed that a change to the mild, sedative air of Pau might now be a judicious move. The event proved otherwise; and, referring to letters now by my side, which I received on his arrival at Pau, I am struck to see how soon the change of air seemed to produce a bad effect. Languor of system, inability to take the cod-liver oil, loss of appetite and increase of debility, were the prominent symptoms, while, at the same time, the expectoration and cough increased, and things turned quite for the worse. In this instance the patient felt convinced he should do better, and feel his chest easier, in a milder air than that of Cannes, but I shall not be soon persuaded again to to let a phthisical invalid, who is feeding well and gradually gaining bodily strength, go from a dry, bracing air to one that is relaxing and mild, because he may at times fancy the former to be rather trying to his chest. In the instance of another patient of whom I have lately heard, a similar change was followed by quite as unfavourable a result.

The change from such a climate as that of Cannes to the sedative air of Pau is a decided one for an invalid, as will be seen by comparing the climate of Pau with that of Cannes, Nice, Hyères, and Provence generally, and this will bring us to consider the effect of bracing climates over pulmonary disease.

CHAPTER V.

Dry and bracing climates—South of France—Nice, Cannes, Hyères—Illustration of good effects of air of Cannes—Sea air at Cannes apt to irritate—Mentone, St. Remo, Malaga, Upper Egypt and the Nile—Illustrative cases—Climates of Norway, Canada and Australia.

In proceeding now to speak of climates that are dry and bracing, with more or less stimulant character in the air, I will take first that part of the South of France known as Provence and the district of the Riviera, where the climate is dry, stimulating, and tonic, possessing a high curative power over a large number of cases of disease of the lungs, as well as of the glandular and lymphatic system.

The general nature of this climate of Provence, lying east of Toulon, is that of a dry, warm air, with more or less of stimulating and exciting quality; an admirable climate for cases of phthisis and chronic bronchitis, attended with copious exhausting discharge, and much general atony of system, but severely trying to nervous and excitable persons, bringing on often an actual attack of nervous fever in those who do not modify their habits of diet and regimen to suit the peculiarities of this exciting climate.

For young children with languid circulation, pallid faces and tendency to glandular enlargements, this climate is strikingly beneficial; also in many cases of atonic dyspepsia with hypochondriasis and rheumatic tendency, the salutary effects of the air of this part of the coast, and especially of Nice, are well displayed.

For pulmonary cases I consider Cannes and Hyères to be superior in most respects to Nice, for of the individual places along this coast, it is in the part of Nice lying nearest the sea that the most exciting air is found, and here, too, the temperature is apt to vary suddenly and considerably, so that it does not appear the best of places for the pulmonary invalid. A patient who had passed a short time at Nice for the benefit of a pulmonary complaint, told me not long ago, that on quitting the place for Cannes, she found after crossing the Var, the air so much more agreeable to her chest, that she could not help remarking to her companions on the ease and comfort she felt; a foreigner, who seemed to have made the journey before in company with English invalids, told her he had frequently heard similar expressions of relief from those who were quitting Nice for the somewhat milder air of Cannes and Hyères.

At these two last-named places, and especially at Hyères, we find an air, dry, warm, and exciting, but more equable and not so highly stimulant as the air of Nice. It is an air eminently suitable to cases of phthisis attended with profuse secretion and much langour and exhaustion of system; it is moreover highly beneficial to cases attended with sluggish circulation and tendency to glandular enlargements and tumours.

Dr. McCarthy, of Paris, has informed me of a lady under his care for most obstinate swelling and ulceration, some considered even of malignant kind, of the cervical glands, who obtained a complete cure after a few months spent at Cannes.

In cases of confirmed and advanced phthisis the effect of the air of Cannes, as a climate intermediate between Hyères and Nice, is most satisfactory, many cases recovering completely from a most serious state of chest disease. M. Girard, the chief Parmacien of Cannes, was in his youth, when a student in Paris, given over by Louis as a case of hopeless phthisis, and advised, as he valued his life, to migrate to the south; he did so, and is now strong and healthy, and while carrying on a large business at Cannes, has found time to write a work "Cannes et ses Environs," in which will be found much useful information from the pen of Dr. J. C. Séve, and also from that of Dr. Whitley, the English physician at Cannes. Speaking of Cannes, Dr. Séve, says; "*Il semble vraiment que cette résidence ait été crée tout exprés pour les poitrinaires, lymphatiques, et scrofuleux;*" and he records several instances of remarkable and permanent recovery that he has seen effected by this climate in most severe cases of consumption.

Some of these patients, it is noticed, were quite unable to remain, though but for a few hours, near to the sea, for the air even of a calm tideless sea like the Mediterranean, seemed too irritating and exciting for them; it caused cough, pain, and hæmoptysis, all of which unpleasant symptoms where relieved as soon as the patient got among the pine woods on the surrounding hills.

The late Dr. Davis remarked, long ago, how the people of Provence and Nice always removed their pulmonic invalids from the sea coast to place them among the pine forests on the hills, where they might inhale the balsamic emanations from these trees.

In all places where the sea is much agitated by winds it is advisable for those with delicate and susceptible lungs to be placed some little distance away from the immediate line of coast; for the saline particles of spray inhaled too freely, cause irritation and often actual hæmoptysis. This would especially hold with respect to the Mediterranean, for although it is a tideless sea and usually calm, yet it contains much more saline matter than the sea of the ocean, therefore the air blowing from it would be highly impregnated with saline particles.

Chemical analysis shews that the water of the ocean, taken at Havre, contains 32·6 gr. of solids, against 40·7 gr. in an equal quantity of the water of the Mediterranean. The chloride of sodium is as 25 gr. to 27 gr.

In the spring months the "mistral" or north-west wind is often severely felt at Cannes, and also at Hyères; then St. Remo affords a sheltered, but tonic atmosphere, for an invalid to resort to until summer sets in. St. Remo has seemed to me superior in climatic respects to Mentone.

It has been said that Mentone is quite exempt from the "mistral," but this is not the case; for when Dr. Madden was at Mentone, in the month of March, this wind had been prevailing for some time.

The air of Mentone is warm and yet bracing, and so clear that the mountains of Corsica, 120 miles off, are frequently seen with the naked eye. The following are notes of temperature recorded by "a wanderer" at Mentone during the last winter, together with other observations so important and true, that I have felt it right to make a few extracts from a letter which appeared in the Times during June 1868.

"A careful register for night and day from January to the middle of March gives the following results according to Fahrenheit:—The lowest night temperature on the north side for January was 34, on the 7th; highest 49, January 22 and 26. It was below 40 on the nights of January 3, 4, 5, 6, and 7. The lowest day temperature on the north side in January was 42, on the 1st, 4th, and 8th; the highest, 56, on the 18th and 27th. It was never lower than 50 for 18 days in January in the shade. For February the lowest night range was 42, on the 19th, when rain fell; the highest, 52, on the 27th. For 23 nights it varied only from 44 to 47. The day temperature for February in the shade was—highest, 58, on the 27th and 28th; lowest 50, on the 22d. On 22 days it ranged from 53 to 58. Rain and snow fell on only four days in January—viz. on the 3d, 4th, 6th, and 8th. There were 17 days with more or less bright and cloudless sky, and nine days cloudy, but fair. February was a brilliant month; rain fell only on the 19th and 22d. Nineteen days were hot, sunny, and cloudless; six cloudy, but fair and cool. Up to the middle of March the night temperature varied from 42 to 49, and that in the day from 50 to 64, except on the 11th and 12th, when, in consequence of heavy rain, it fell to 46."

"As a general rule, it may be said that the hotels and villas at Mentone are all exposed, in a greater or less degree, to the noxious influences arising from the state of the drains and from the inexcusable neglect of those ordinary decencies and comforts inside the dwellings which in England have long been considered to be matters of course in civilized life, but which are as yet but very imperfectly appreciated on the Continent. The purity and dryness of the atmosphere, and the important fact that the water supply is derived not from wells, but is brought in aqueducts from the mountains, may be the reason that Mentone has escaped the visitations of the cholera. But as the town increases how long will this immunity continue? What is to be done with the sewage? Will the purity of the air be maintained as new lines of houses and of cesspools stretch along the eastern and western bays? These questions can only be answered by those whose material interests depend upon the continued popularity of Mentone. They are vital ones, and they cannot be long postponed, or if so Dr. Bennet's pretty swallow may be driven to a longer flight than from England to Mentone. As a residence this place is expensive—quite as much, or perhaps even more so than Nice or Cannes. The hotel charges and rents for villas are, for the most part, unreasonably high, nor is the quality of the food equal to that in many places where prices are lower. There are some good-looking *pensions* in different parts of the town, and at some of these I believe visitors are accommodated on more reasonable terms; but the villas generally are inferior and uncomfortable. They are for the most part badly built, badly ventilated, with doors and windows ill-made and rarely draught proof. They are, in fact, run up for as little as possible, so as to pay the owners probably 15 per cent., or more. The floors are usually made with red hexagonal tiles, and the furniture is like the house in quality, and barely sufficient in quantity. There are some houses of a better class here, which are built and furnished more in accordance with comfort, but they are few and far between. Nothing is more wanted at Mentone than houses of a more comfortable character and better suited for English families, who have to pay rents absurdly high for very inferior accommodation. There is a custom in taking a villa to which special attention should be directed. The house is let furnished, and generally stands in a garden of moderate size. Having signed the agreement and taken possession, you make the unpleasant discovery, after a few days, that your tenancy is limited to the walls of the house. The garden or enclosure with its walks and flower beds, and which you unsuspiciously looked upon as part of your take, is purposely left out of the agreement, and the landlord and his family or friends claim and exercise the right and ownership up to the doors and windows, coming and going at all hours, and telling you that the flowers are theirs, and that you can only pluck them by permission. The privacy of the dwelling is of course destroyed, and besides that, the unlucky visitors have been in several instances subjected to serious insult and annoyance. No one should sign an agreement without insisting upon the garden being included saving the right of the owner to the crop of olives or lemons therein. The railway from Nice to Genoa passes through Mentone, and the works progress rapidly; when finished it will be a great boon to the public. There are several places further on towards Genoa and Spezzia favourably situated for building, and well adapted for invalids, all of which will be more easily reached from England when the line is open than this place is, now that the terminus is at Nice. As new resorts for travellers spring up along the Riviera the wholesome effects of competition will not fail to produce their results, and the Mentonese must be prepared to encounter the rivalry of such places as Alassio, Rappallo, Sestri, and Spezzia, where equally favourable conditions, both of climate and situation, prevail, with mountain scenery as beautiful and in some respects almost surpassing that of Mentone." *Times*, June, 1868.

The season of Mentone lasts from October to May.

I must refer my reader for further details respecting the places along this part of the French and

Italian coast to some of the works given in the note below,* and from them ample information can be well obtained. I have named, and shortly described those health resorts along this coast, where I am convinced a large class of invalids really obtain a true renewal of life and strength, and I have passed over other places; as for instance, Florence, and Naples, for such experience as I have been able to gain would lead me to dissuade any consumptive invalid from going thither to regain lost health.

With respect to the general immunity of the district of Provence and the Riviera from phthisis, I would just quote the experience of M. Richelmi, who for thirty-four years practised among its inhabitants; he reckons the population of Monaco, Mentone, Villefranche, and St. Remo, and some other places on the coast, to amount to 76,000 souls, and of 7,000 deaths in this number, only 107 where due to pulmonary consumption.

Dr. Chambers, in his very interesting book on the climate of Italy, says, that while in London 1 death in 8 is due to consumption, in Genoa the proportion is 1 in 13, and even that Dr. Du Jardin considers unusually high.

Asthma and Bronchitis cause in Genoa, 1 death in 20, while in London the proportion is 1 in 10.

To show, on the other hand, how unsuitable this

---

* Dr. T. M. Madden on *Change of Climate.—A Guide to France, Spain, Italy, Egypt etc.*—Dr. C. T. Williams on *Climate of South of France.*—Dr. Prosser James on *St. Remo and Mentone.*—Third edition of Dr. J. Henry Bennet's work on *South of Europe.*

bracing climate is for those who have an inflammatory tendency, Dr. Chambers tells us that acute affections of the respiratory organs caused in Genoa 1 death in 9, and in London 1 in 16.

Acute inflammations of the nervous centres caused in Genoa 1 death in 59; in London 1 in 119.

These statistics fully bear out previous remarks as to the class of patient, for whom the clear bracing air of Provence and Italy is manifestly injurious. The climate is a decided one, powerful alike for good or evil, and like all powerful remedies must be used with proper precautions.

Other dry, bracing, and stimulating climates, somewhat similar to those we have just been describing, may be met with at Malaga, Malta, and Algiers. I have heard phthisical people speak very highly of these climates, but the absence of the usual comforts of home has been named as a drawback; an annoyance that, in the case of confirmed invalids, outweighs any peculiar advantages of climate.

Dr. Madden, after passing more than one winter at Malaga, observes that the dry tonic air of the place will work wonders in most cases of incipient consumption, with cachectic and languid state of the system; many cases too where the disease is advanced will, for a time, improve in a remarkable way at Malaga.

In irritative bronchitis the air is, as we should expect, too dry and exciting, and it is a perilous place for those affected with this kind of complaint; in humoral asthma, on the other hand, and in bronchitis with much secretion, enfeebled and degenerative capillaries and much general relaxation of system, the air of Malaga is likely to suit admirably.

The mean annual temperature of Malaga is 65°, or 15° higher than London, 9° higher than Pau, and 7° lower than Cairo. In winter the mean is 55°, being the same as Algiers, and the summer mean is 78°, this being one degree higher than Algiers, and 8°, higher than Pau.

At Cannes the mean annual temperature is 60°, and in January, the coldest month, the thermometer keeps very steady between 46°, and 48°. The annual number of rainy days at Cannes is 52, at Hyéres 40, and at Nice 60, hence invalids have abundant opportunity for being out of doors, a point of much moment to them in promoting their cure.

An eminently dry, warm, and stimulating climate is that of Cairo; this part of Egypt may be resorted to by young persons, in whom incipient phthisis is slowly and insidiously progressing, with every prospect of great benefit, but in cases where there is liability to febrile attacks, and pulmonary congestion with dry hard cough and frequent hæmoptysis, the climate is far too exciting.

The best time of the year for Cairo is from October to March. The climate of the Nile generally as far as Thebes, which is 300 miles south east of Cairo, is warm, dry, and equable, though at times cold winds are felt, and the patient on arriving first at the river is apt to suffer from transient disturbance of the digestive and biliary functions, especially if, in spite of the wise advice of Dr. H. Bennet, he has been travelling in the "cannon ball style," making the transition from one climate to another with more haste than wisdom; but, when used with reasonable precautions, the climate of the Nile can do much certainly towards overcoming a very decided tuberculous tendency in the chest, as I have observed in more than one well-marked instance.

In advanced phthisis with ulceration of the lungs, I should by no means advise an invalid to get as far from home as Upper Egypt, for any good the climate might do him.

In the two following cases it will be observed how the patients, both of whom were injuriously affected by mild and humid climates, got great benefit from change to the dry air of Upper Egypt—one was the case of a clergyman afflicted with most severe and persistent bronchitic asthma, and utter loss of all appetite and strength, to whom the air of Cairo and the Thebaid proved most beneficial, though by the moist air of Alexandria this patient's distress was much increased, and his dyspepsia seriously aggravated. Another phthisical patient, whose sufferings were aggravated during a winter at Madeira, removed to the Thebaid with most prompt and decided benefit. —See Rev. T. Barclay, in *Edinburgh Medical and Surgical Journal*, 1854, p. 656.

I am able, since writing the last edition of this book, to bear testimony to the truly curative effect of the air of Upper Egypt in two cases of young men affected with very decided signs of consumption in the upper part of one lung. One of these, now an officer in the Army, remains so well, that atmospheric changes are of small moment to him; the other, an engineer, is sure to have a return of his cough if he is exposed to an atmosphere that is at all damp. While speaking here of bracing climates I would draw attention to Norway and Canada, as fine summer climates for the consumptive; of the effect of the air of Norway on those with a tendency to phthisis I am able to speak most favourably. In Canada the air is cold, but very dry and bracing.

Many of the Australian climates are spoken highly of as suiting well consumptive people. Dr. Dongan Bird describes these climates as temperate and dry and yet unirritating to susceptible chests. In Victoria the mortality from phthisis is not one quarter of what it is in Great Britain.

In Tasmania the climate is sedative and rather moist.

CHAPTER VI.

On the more bracing climates of Great Britain—Causes of the variable nature of English climates—West coast of Scotland—Examples shewing the curative effects of the bracing air of the east coast of England in cases of confirmed phthisis.—Signs of convalescence indicated by the cough—Places on the coast possessing a tonic and bracing air—Scarborough, Yarmouth, Cromer, Margate, Folkestone, Weymouth, The Channel Islands—Bracing climates found inland—Harrogate, Malvern, Buxton, Clifton, &c.

HAVING in Chapter IV. made mention of those parts of England where an air that is of a sedative and mild character is best obtained, I purpose now in the present chapter to speak of some of those places where a tonic and bracing air is met with in the greatest perfection. The line of demarcation between the two groups of climatic resorts is one that is not sharply drawn, for if we take Torquay as the representative of a perfectly sedative and mild climate, and Harrogate as presenting the other extreme of a dry, bracing, and highly tonic, climate, we can easily find places possessing, what we may call intermediate qualities, being warm, and yet at the same time free from that relaxing effect on the system which characterizes so many of the climates which are known as being both warm and sedative. I should be disposed to speak of Ventnor, Clifton, Cheltenham and St. Leonards as examples of intermediate climates; free from marked relaxing tendency and yet not possessing the high tonic power of such places as Harrogate, Malvern, or Weymouth.

Reference to the following description of the climate of the British Islands, as given by Professor Daniell in his Meteorological Essays, will shew why it is that the climate of these Islands is so uncertain and variable, and therefore not well adapted for people with delicate chests.

"The British Islands are so situated as to be subject to all the circumstances which can possibly be supposed to render a climate irregular and variable. Placed nearly in the centre of the temperate zone, where the range of temperature is very great, their atmosphere is subject, on the one side to the impressions of the largest continent in the world; and on the other to those of the vast Atlantic Ocean. Upon their coasts the great stream of aqueous vapour, perpetually rising from the western waters, first receives the influence of the land whence emanate those condensations and expansions which deflect and reverse the grand system of equipoised currents. They are also within the reach of the frigorific effects of the immense barriers and fields of ice, which, when the shifting position of the sun advances the tropical climate towards the northern pole, counteract its energy, and present a condensing surface of immense extent to the increasing elasticity of the aqueous atmosphere."

Such are the scientific explanations of that well-known variability of the climate of Great Britain which causes so many English invalids to forsake their own country and seek some of those warmer and more equable climates to be found in other quarters of the globe.

Notwithstanding these serious objections to a climate that is variable and often visited by damp and cold fogs, there are nevertheless to be found in the Islands of Britain climates that can do great things towards not only relieving, but actually curing pulmonary disease. The sedative climates have been already noticed, we now consider those that are bracing and somewhat cold.

Among the bracing climates of the British Isles, I should place the west coast of Scotland, where, as we have seen, consumption is an unknown disease; and a summer spent in sailing among the islands there would be a remedy well worth the trial of any who could afford such an agreeable and efficacious mode of cure. My own belief is, that a consumptive invalid, after spending all the months of the year from May to September in such a climate as that which exists between Rothsay and the Northern Isles of the Western Hebrides, would find any previous apprehensions he might have been feeling as to where he should winter, reduced to a minimum, so much he would have gained in health, strength, and spirits, during the summer thus spent.

One patient of mine, who for many years has carried about what appears to be a small cavity in the right lung, finds no climate in England, or elsewhere, to agree so perfectly with him as an Island on the west coast of Scotland. It appears to me that the unsound lung has demonstrably improved during a long summer spent in this island. On removing south last winter this patient had an attact of hæmoptysis, but it was slighter than previous attacks had been and soon passed off.

Those for whom the West of Scotland does not seem good, are persons with any tendency to diarrhœa or dysentery.

From what I have observed of the effect of the strongly bracing air of the Yorkshire, and Norfolk coasts, in cases of genuine phthisis, I cannot but think highly of these parts, as strikingly beneficial during summer to the consumptive; while in the winter even, they are not so hazardous as might by some be thought. Not very long ago I had an opportunity of seeing consumption fairly in its second stage in both lungs arrested in a most extraordinary way, by the patient going and fearlessly encountering, the east winds of spring on the coast of Norfolk.

The patient, when I saw him, was expectorating much, had a languid circulation, but good appetite and plenty of nerve and spirit. The physical signs on both sides of the chest were so marked and serious, that I feared to let him go far from town and advised Tunbridge Wells, as a dry and bracing place near London; however he went off to the east coast of Norfolk, and I have seldom seen pulmonary symptoms so promptly and decidedly checked by any remedy as they were in this case by a strong and bracing air.

During this gentleman's residence on the East coast he completely lost his cough and profuse expectoration, and gained in appetite and in flesh, although the expansive movement of the chest walls was notably diminished, and resonance on percussion was much impaired.

He remained well for near two years, and then, I was informed, he got, while in London, a severe attack of double pneumonia which carried him off.

While I have been employed in writing these pages I have attended a young lady who, when first I saw her, was hardly able to turn in bed, was worn fearfully thin, had signs of softening tubercle at the right apex, while the left lung seemed to me to be one large cavity. I hardly expected her to live many weeks, but after she had taken the Hypophosphite of Lime for a time she was not only able to come down stairs, but soon was strong enough to bear a journey out to the north side of London beyond Hampstead to a highly bracing air. After residing there for a time she went to Yarmouth and now, by my advice, is going to St. Leonards, improved to a degree I could scarcely have believed possible in so short a period of time. An interesting and marked feature in this case is the supervention of a troublesome dry irritating cough coincidently with the improvement in the lung symptoms, this is the cough of phthisical convalescence to which both Dr. Hughes Bennett and Dr. Henry Bennet have drawn attention, the latter at page 40 of his admirable remarks on Pulmonary Consumption. The real remedy for this cough is not to give opiates or expectorants but to cause the patient to repress the effort at coughing until the natural action of the bronchial villi has pushed the little collection of muco-pus, which causes the irritation, into the larynx, whence it can be easily expelled. Another patient of mine now passing her second winter at Mentone, and who has arrested phthisical disease in her right lung, presents this description of cough exactly; she has taken various sedatives and expectorants without much relief, so that now she pays little attention to it.

During the summer, and early autumn, few better situations can be found for consumptive persons, who prefer the sea coast, than some of the well-known watering places on the East coast of England.

Scarborough and its vicinity may be mentioned as one of the best situations on the coast; although both places are bracing, yet, as compared with Whitby and some places further north on the Coast, I judge Scarborough to be the best place on the Yorkshire coast for the residence of one who is consumptive.

On the Norfolk coast, Yarmouth, and Cromer, as well as Lowestoft are well-known places where a bracing air is met with, and the good that this kind of climate can do to some cases of confirmed and even advanced consumption has been already proved.

Margate is a place suitable to many of the consumptive, but practical experience has shewn me that there is a peculiar keenness in the air, during a considerable part of the year, that is neither agreeable nor yet beneficial to those who have established lung disease.

Those who have complained of the air of Margate and its neighbourhood not suiting them, I have advised to remove to Folkestone, and have found the move an exceedingly good one. It has occurred to me that the nature of the soil must make a difference in these cases. Margate, and the Isle of Thanet generally, is on the Chalk, while Folkestone is on the green sand, where this joins a band of gault. The same difference of soil obtains in the case of Brighton as compared with St. Leonards, the first being on chalk, the other on sand, and I believe most persons will say with me that St. Leonards agrees with pulmonic patients much better than Brighton does.

On the Dorsetshire coast is Weymouth a place long noted for its salubrity, so that it has been said no physician could live or die at Weymouth. Eastward of Weymouth, opposite to Bournemouth, is the bay of Swanage with a fine bracing climate, good as a change in summer from the hot beach of Bournemouth. Swanage appears to be rising in repute as a health resort, and it seems from such returns as are to be met with, that the mortality from consumption at Swanage is very small.

We are told by a writer in the Medical Times for October the 10th 1868, that the population of the parish of Swanage was 2139 in 1851, and 2004 in 1861. In 1866 the deaths from all causes were 34; in 1867, during which year the whooping cough carried off many children, the deaths mere 42. The deaths from pulmonary consumption were five in each of these years.

Closeness in the apartments of the dwelling houses, and habits of intermarriage, are spoken of, by the writer above quoted, as causes in powerful action to impair the vitality of the natives.

From Weymouth the channel islands are soon reached, and form excellent marine climates for invalids till far into the autumn. The mean Temperature of the Isle of Guernsey is 51·50° F. The winter temperature being 44·2. Spring, 47·7. Summer 59·9. Autumn 53·8. For some of those affected with true asthma the highly marine air of these islands has seemed to me unsuitable.

Having thus pointed out in the foregoing short notices some of the bracing marine climates of England, I would now mention some of the bracing climates found inland, for often it happens that a patient cannot bear a marine climate so well as one that is inland; the former, in certain cases, causing nausea more or less persistent, with disturbance of the biliary organs; in these cases a situation removed to a distance from the sea coast is indicated.

Among the inland climates of England we have at Malvern, Harrogate and Buxton, climates that I would most strongly commend to the consumptive. One patient of mine with confirmed tubercular disease in both lungs of many years standing, lives on the strength of the draughts of vitalizing air which the diseased lungs obtain from time to time at Malvern. Were this patient to go to a relaxing climate I doubt if she would live three months; it would be with her as with a phthisical invalid I saw flourishing well at Harrogate, and who told me how some of the highest London authorities ordered him to Torquay. "I felt" he said "that had I stayed there a mouth I should not have left the place alive". His case clearly was one requiring a bracing air and his own instinct seemed to have guided him to Harrogate.

Torquay was resorted to as being "a place good for consumption" and the case is a parallel one with that related to me by my friend Dr. Symes Thompson of the Brompton Hospital, where a patient, apparently cured of phthisis by the bracing air of the South of France, several years subsequently had all the evil symptoms return on going for a winter to Torquay; a removal northward was soon followed by improvement.

At Harrogate the patient has the advantage of the dry bracing air of High Harrogate blowing over the sandy soil of the "Stray" or common, or if this air be too strong he can easily migrate to the more sheltered part of Low Harrogate.

Of the well-known Harrogate waters it is not my purpose here to speak. We know that the saline sulphur water of Eaux Bonnes in France is resorted to in cases of very chronic phthisis, and I doubt not the sulphur water of Harrogate will be found at times useful, but all the sulphur waters must be used with extreme caution by consumptive people and only under careful medical supervision.*

Buxton in Derbyshire is a good bracing climate from June till October. The elevation of this district to 900 feet above the sea level renders the air especially pure, and forms a very strong recommendation to Buxton. For information as to the Buxton waters and what use they may have to the consumptive I must refer people to Dr. Robertson, and his book on Buxton and its waters.

Among other inland climates Clifton is one that is dry and moderately bracing. I cannot from the observed effect of the air on the consumptive testify to its curative effects as I can in the cases of the more decidedly bracing places.

In one case of a patient with rather advanced phthisis, who went by his own wish to Clifton during a warm part of the year, it seemed as if the change thither tended to accelerate the fatal event.

---

* Those who desire information as to the Sulphur and Chalybeate waters of Harrogate will find such in the works of the late Dr. Kennion and also of Dr. Myrtle.

CHAPTER VII.

Illustrations of the curative effect of a bracing air in advanced pulmonary disease—Opinions of numerous physicians and others confirming the authors views on this point—Curative effect of an open air life for those in advanced consumption—Practical conclusions and suggestions.

The short notices of different health resorts, of name and repute, that have been given in the foregoing pages, have been intended merely to point out the general features of the climate and to illustrate its effects on the different kinds and stages of pulmonary disease, and not to serve as regular, and special descriptions, of each place individually.

The point I have been most anxious to make clear is, that because a place is very sheltered, with a warm, humid, and relaxing air, it is not necessarily for these reasons to be at once set down as a first-rate place for all who are consumptive, and that the more advanced the stage of the disease the more important it is for the enfeebled patient to be kept closely to one of these warm relaxing languid spots. Far from this being the case I believe that the only chance of life for one who being decidedly in an advancing consumption, is not getting better, and perhaps getting worse, in a warm air, is at once to make a change to a bracing and colder air, and not to fear if at first he may possibly have a little increase of cough and tightness at the chest for a day or two after making the change.

The cases in which I have known decidedly curative effects to be produced by a strong and bracing air, have been those of persons very far gone, according to good authority, in phthisis, and who had been sent to the mildest and most relaxing parts of the English coast, in the belief that there alone they could exist. One case obtained permission to go for the hot months of the summer to a very exposed and cold part of Hertfordshire, intending to leave for Rome in the winter; the effect of the summer air was so renovating to the exhausted system, that the patient remained in the same spot all through the winter, appetite and strength returned, and by the next summer complete recovery had taken place.

In another case a patient who was dying of phthisis, in the most sheltered part of Hastings, left to go to her home in Lancashire with but little hope of continuing her existence; she got perfectly well, and probably remains so now, after the lapse of several years.

I could without difficulty add to the list of those, who being far advanced in consumption, have made most extraordinary recoveries on going, for the first time during the course of their illness, into a cool and bracing atmosphere.

It is not long since Professor Laycock of Edinburgh, when telling me of the rapidity with which he got rid of a very obstinate chronic bronchitis, with copious secretion, in the dry bracing air of Yorkshire, related to me a highly interesting case of a young gentleman, very far gone in consumption, on whose case the opinion of Dr. Laycock was requested. It seemed that this young man had seen more than one eminent lung doctor in London, and all agreed that his only chance of continued existence lay in his at once going abroad for the winter. The difficulty was to decide where he should go, since while one physician advised one place in most urgent terms, another in equally strong terms condemned it as quite unsuitable to the requirements of the case under consideration.

The case being placed before Dr. Laycock, he proposed that the patient should remain at his own house in Yorkshire, and although this proposal was not acquiesced in without some surprise, and perhaps a little doubt, it was nevertheless eventually carried out. The happy result was that the patient recovered health and strength in a way, and to an extent, which astounded all who saw him, and the improvement appears, after the lapse of some years, to be still permanent.

Having, in the preface to the Second Edition of this work, made the remark that the views set forth are not entirely new, and by no means peculiar to the author alone, I wish here to quote the words of men of no light authority in the profession of physic that it may be seen how far their sentiments accord with my own.

Thus, Baron Larrey, the great Army Surgeon of Napoleon I., has gone so far as to say "that it is a fatal error or rather a pernicious prejudice, to imagine that warm mild climates cure pulmonic disease. In the advanced stages of phthisis, atmospheric heat does harm, and accelerates the fatal issue."—*Med. Chir. Rev.*, 1845, p. 59.

With the phthisical out-patients at Victoria Park Hospital, I have been much struck to see how much better they seemed to be during the frosts of the winter than during the languid heat of August. Dr. Risdon Bennett has informed me that this is the general experience of the physicians of the hospital.

"The warmest of our summers are as injurious to the consumptive, especially the advanced cases, as the cold of winter," says Dr. Wood of Philadelphia.

Dr. Chapman, of the same city, says "I am well persuaded that to the consumptive the effects of intense heat are more baneful than those of severe cold."—*Wood's Practice of Medicine.* vol. II. p. 93.

Dr. Henry Bennet says, "a moist, mild climate should be avoided as calculated to depress vitality" and "consumptive persons are rather damaged than improved by such a climate."

In Dr. Tanner's Practice of Medicine (5th edition) in some remarks by Dr. Burgess on the climate of Rome, Dr. B points out "that the popular feeling in favour of a mild and relaxing climate in consumption is altogether wrong, being based upon erroneous data, if not mere tradition." "A cold climate, (continues Dr. Burgess) such as that of Norway or Canada, with a still air, is a more rational indication if the formation of tubercle, is the result of a relaxed state of the vital functions, involving impaired digestion, depraved nutrition, and degeneration of the blood. Nothing is more calculated to derange the digestive organs than the sedative influence of a relaxing or malarious atmosphere. The mild climate allays bronchial irritation at the expense of the general health and nutrition."

Dr. Fuller, after proving by decisive statistics, that England is considered solely in reference to its mortality from consumption will bear comparison with any other equally civilized country, remarks (page 405 of Fuller on Diseases of the Lungs 2nd Edit.) how " the consumptive out-door patient of a hospital coming in all weathers to the hospital for his medicine notoriously lives longer than his brother who, more fortunate in being well fed and protected from the inclemency of the weather, is shut up in the equably heated wards of the hospital, and thus loses the bracing and invigorating stimulus of the fresh breezes of heaven." This is perfectly true, if the in-patient of the hospital be literally shut up merely in warm wards and corridors, and the remark shews what an inestimable advantage a large cheerfully arranged garden is to a consumption hospital; such as can be seen at the Victoria Park Hospital where the patients can have daily exercise in a pure and healthy atmosphere.

As a sign of the times, and indication of how popular, as well as professional feeling is tending to the treatment of consumption by pure and bracing air, I could not but observe the following passage in the "Times" of December 3rd 1866, when commenting on the trial of Hunter v. Sharp.

The words were these,—

"It was, for instance, the received doctrine some twenty years ago that a relaxing atmosphere was most favorable to the recovery of consumptive patients; but subsequent experience, we believe, has greatly modified this opinion."

The curative effect of an open air life in cases of true and advanced consumption has been most strikingly exemplified by Dr. J. Blake.

In the *Brit.* and *For. Med. Chir. Review* for July, 1864, it is told how Dr. James Blake, of San Francisco, caused seven consumptive patients to spend a whole summer constantly in the open air at an elevation of from 3000 to 5000 feet above the level of the sea, in a region where no rain falls for 5 or 6 months; they ate, drank and slept out of doors, literally "*sub Jove*," and all gained in weight and in strength, and seem to have been cured, though previously the usual remedies had been tried without benefit.

Such being the beneficial effect of open air life, we must endeavour to find a climate where the invalid can, without undue pain and distress to his chest, and without risk of getting wet and chilled, be much in the open air, and then the more bracing the air that can be borne without discomfort the better.

To ensure a good chance of being much out of doors, an invalid should endeavour to ascertain the average number of rainy days in the year at the place whither he purposes to go, and should also find to some extent how the temperature varies. Merely to know the mean temperature is of little use, for two places may differ very widely in their extremes and yet may both have the same mean; hence the amount of variation should be noticed between morning and midday, and day and night, and the less difference there is between the out-door, and in-door, temperature the better.

Other matters requiring attention, especially by those going abroad, are, the accommodation afforded to invalids, the nature and kind of food to be obtained, &c.; for without attention to these matters the life of an invalid abroad will be one of utter misery and wretchedness. From what I have myself seen of serious cases of consumption that I have met with abroad seeking relief in foreign lands, I would earnestly advise that no really bad, and advanced cases of that disease, should try a climate distant from home unless able to take with them, friends, servants and physician to be constantly at hand.

In conclusion, I would commend the study of climate and its effects on invalids, pulmonary and other, to the investigation of those, who in these days of facile locomotion, are led to visit various parts of our own and other countries.

We want more experiments on the cases of actual invalids, just such as were made with the patients sent out to make trial of the climate of Madeira. In process of time we may hope that the records of the Sanatoria, and invalid homes, which exist at St.

Leonards, Bournemouth, Ventnor, Weston-super-Mare, and other places, may be turned to some good practical account in guiding us in our climatic treatment of pulmonary patients.

Mere meteorological observations and elaborate tables of temperature, interesting and to a certain extent useful as they doubtless are, should not be the exclusive means of investigation, but to these should be added carefully recorded results of the way in which invalids eat, drink, and thrive, under certain conditions of climate, "as yet we are," to quote the words of Dr. Walshe, "wanting in precise observations on invalids themselves, and till this want be supplied, attempts at fixing the climate fittest for any particular form of disease must often result in disappointment. Nevertheless, some general truths have been acquired to guide us, and one of the most important of these appears to be, that the anatomical condition and presumed intimate nature of the affection are less faithful guides than the state of the organism generally, and the liking of the individual, in the selection of a dry and bracing or a moist and relaxing climate."

CHAPTER VIII.

On the Diet and Digestion of pulmonary patients—Importance of exercise to ensure proper assimilation of Nutriment—Various kinds of food and drink—Preparations of Iceland Moss—Use of Whey—Diet under special circumstances—Of habits of life, exercise, sleep, Turkish bath, and cold bathing—Peculiar feeling of weakness, not a bad sign—Concluding remarks.

Sir James Clark, in his treatise on Climate, (page 245) says, " I would strongly advise every person who goes abroad for the recovery of health, whatever be his disease, or to whatever climate he may go, to consider the change as merely placing him in a condition the most favourable for the removal of his disease, and to bear constantly in mind that the beneficial influence of travelling, of sailing, and of climate, require to be aided by such a regimen and mode of living, and by such remedial measures, as would have been necessary had the invalid remained at home."

Without due attention to this advice the effect of the best chosen climate may prove disappointing to both patient and physician, and as an endeavour towards the prevention of such mischance, I have thought it would not be out of place here to append a short chapter on the diet and regimen of pulmonary patients; for with these, as indeed with all who are affected by a chronic disease, attention to the stomach and digestive organs is a matter of paramount importance. The following remarks are designed to be short, and as much to the point as possible; more ample information can be well obtained from those recent treatises, which have within the last few years, come forth from the medical press at the hands of the Drs. E. Smith, Richardson, and Horace Dobell.

Patients, generally, are pretty well impressed with the importance of endeavouring to overcome the debility consequent upon the inroads of consumptive disease by taking into the system plenty of food of the most nutritious kind, but in doing this they have not always due regard to the capabilities of the digestive organs for rightly disposing of the mass of nutrient matter with which they are loaded.

Too often, in these cases, the oppressed stomach is goaded to put forth extraordinary efforts by a very free allowance of alcoholic stimulants, and when there is a quantity of semi-digested aliment lying in the stomach there is no doubt that steeping this in alcohol tends to prevent, to some extent, fermentation, flatulence, and acidity, and thus gives relief to uncomfortable feelings; but taken in this extensive way alcohol rather retards, than promotes, the healthy digestion of the food.

The great point to bear in mind, while using our best endeavours to sustain the strength by means of nutritious food, is, that the body generally is nourished by what is digested and preperly assimilated, and not merely by the amount of nutrient matter that can be stowed away in the stomach.

Some, unquestionably, make better blood and build up firmer tissues, from a diet of milk, eggs, and farinaceous food, than they do when they are fully supplied with all manner of flesh meats and plenty of alcoholic drinks; so that in arranging the dietary of an invalid, the general state and constitution must be considered, and that food will prove most nutritious which is most acceptable to the stomach and most easily digested therein.

Another point to be borne in mind, is, that a man digests with his arms, legs, and lungs, as well as with his stomach.

Air and exercise cause the assimilation of nutrient matter into healthy tissues, and, without these two important adjuvants to perfect digestion, much unassimilated nutrient matter is expelled from the body in the nitrogen of the fœces (as has been well proved by Dr. Edward Smith in his experiment on prisoners) or, if retained, is only converted into some of the products of unhealthy and imperfect metamorphosis such as the lithic acid of Gout, or the quasi-fibrinous matter of Tubercle and Struma, the first of these depositing as chalk stones of lithate of soda in the joints, the second in the lungs causing their destruction by softening, and the third more rarely in the lungs, but often in the bones, joints, and glandular system, leading likewise to the destruction of these parts of the body.

Dr. Gairdner, who lays great stress on respiration as a nutrient process, says, "Aeration of the blood in the lungs is the source of the fibrin; by exercise fibrin is carried forward to the tissues, and by exercise, air, and moderation in diet, such constitutional diseases as Gout, Tubercle, Struma, &c., may be avoided and cured; without these means it is vain to look for more than temporary palliation and suspension of the most acute symptoms of the disease."

To shew how blood globules and fibrin are elaborated, under the influence of free nutrition and active exercise, Dr. Gairdner had three rabbits abundantly fed for many days and their blood examined. Rabbit No. 1 was allowed free exercise, Nos. 2 and 3 were kept confined. It will be seen by the table that while the albumen varied little, the more highly elaborated principles, the globules and the fibrin varied considerably, most fibrin and globules being formed where there was most air and exercise.

	Albumen	Globules	Fibrin	
Rabbit No. 1	50·20	97·40	2·10	in 1000 parts
,, 2	49·	80·50	1·75	
,, 3	48·20	75·43	1·96	

In the Proceedings of the Royal Society, Vol. xii. pp. 399, and 505, Mr. A. H. Smee shews, by experiment, how fibrin is produced by the direct action of oxygen on albumen, this formation of fibrin being accompanied by the evolution of sulphur, phosphorus, and carbonic acid. Mr. Smee shews also how albumen, artificially digested in gastric juice, produces fibrin by its subsequent oxidation.

Gluten too, when oxidized, appears to yield fibrin.

Under the influence of improper diet, and imperfect aeration, it is this fibrinous element of the blood which degenerates into scrofulous, or tuberculous matter and is deposited as such in the various organs of the body as has been stated already.

The close chemical analogy between tubercle and that substance called protein, which forms the basis of the nitrogenous, or flesh-forming elements of nutrition, Albumen, Casein, and Fibrin, is seen in these comparative analyses as given by Dr. J. G. Atkinson, of Wakefield.

	Carbon.	Hydrogen.	Nitrogen.	Oxygen.
Protein	43	35	6	13
Tubercle	48	36	6	14

Tubercle therefore differs but little in chemical composition from that body (Protein) which is looked upon as a most important and essential flesh-forming principle of the system, and the mere loading the stomach with abundance of food will be no protection whatever against the inroads of the worst and most rapid form of consumption unless by due exercise in the air the nutrient matter is properly elaborated and deposited to replace those tissues which are used up, oxydized, and carried out of the body.

A certain amount of waste of tissue is essential to its proper nutrition and renewal, and it is also very essential that the products of the used up and wasted tissue, be properly converted into such bodies as can be carried out of the system by the various emunctories such as the lungs, skin, liver, kidneys &c.

Let all these conditions of waste, removal, and renewal, be well fufilled and the development of tubercle is almost impossible.

To deduce from the foregoing observations such practical conclusions as will enable us to tell each individual how much tissue he wastes per hour, and how much, and what kind of food will exactly compensate him for this waste, is a matter to which none would pretend to attain, and, if attained, would render a pair of scales, a graduated measure, and perhaps sundry other scientific appliances articles absolutely essential at the meals of the invalid. Without going to this extreme however, the researches of scientific men, and among the first of Dr. Edward Smith, have guided us to a good deal that is of practical utility and importance in ordering the diet of patients in various stages of pulmonary disease.

In chronic phthisis, as in all chronic diseases, the first point demanding attention is the state of the digestive functions, and no better criterion of a certain climate agreeing with a patient can be afforded than by his finding the air make him hungry, and his meals render him cheerful and strong.

It is in its depressant action on the digestive and biliary functions that we so often see the highly injurious effect of a warm and humid climate. The liver, an organ which of all others it is most important to maintain in good working order for the purpose of digesting fatty matters, and preventing the acidification of farinaceous food, is very apt to suffer from congestion and torpidity in a hot climate, and while the patient may be full of praise of the mild soft air so soothing to his chest above, the seeds of dysentery and other grievous ills may be in sure preparation in the lower organs of his body.

To one, who while presenting signs of incipient tuberculosis in the lungs, is yet able to take plenty of exercise, and complains little of anything like dyspepsia, I believe that a free and liberal range of diet is not only safe, but advisable, and the less curiously intent the patient is to whatever he puts into his stomach the better; provided always that the food from which selection is made, be of a simple and nutritious kind, excluding rich pastry and all such highly seasoned made dishes as tempt the palate to overload the stomach, thereby doing immense mischief.

With respect to solid animal food, free choice of fish, flesh, and fowl, may be allowed, but whatever be the kind, the more simply it is cooked the better. Thus fish is better boiled than fried, and done thus the various kinds of white fish may be often taken. Shell fish generally are objectionable as being hard of digestion, with the exception of oysters, and these cooked or uncooked are well adapted as an article of diet for the phthisical.

Of meats, beef and mutton should take the first place, and these meats will be better roasted than boiled, care being taken that they are not in either case overdone. Chops and steaks can be stewed occasionally by way of a change.

Of other meats, and of poultry, game and the like, there need not be much said, they form a list from which an invalid need not be debarred should he incline to them. Game in a high condition however, and meats that have been salted are best avoided, the first is apt to cause diarrhœa, and the second is very difficult of digestion and at the same time of small nutritive value to the system.

Among salt meats however an exception should be made in the case of fat bacon; this may be freely given to those able and willing to take it, indeed fat generally being a most important calorific and respiratory food, should enter as much as possible into the diet of the consumptive. Many unfortunately, have a great repugnance to anything in the least degree oily or fatty, while a few can take fat and oils in a way that is astounding. One patient of my own, in the second stage of phthisis, appears as if he could live on the fat of beef, while the smallest piece of meat brings on acute gastric disturbance. I have observed these great consumers of fat and oil stand well against their disease, they are well able to turn to good use the calorific elements of nutrition and thus save excessive waste of tissue; others, less fortunate, turn the fat into butyric, and other noxious acids, and from these it must be withheld, as doing harm rather than good, till the digestive organs have learned to make a better use of it.

With the chief meal of animal food it will not be well to mix much food of vegetable and farinaceous kind, for these substances will distend the stomach and will also absorb much of that gastric juice which is wanted for the perfect digestion in the stomach of the fleshy part of the food.

Hence but little bread, and that stale, or unfermented, and but a moderate quantity of one or two kinds of well cooked vegetables should be taken with the meat, and afterwards nothing more should be allowed than some stewed fruit, roasted apples, or a very small pudding of bread, rice, corn flour, semolina or the like.

Such fruits as grapes, strawberries, and perfectly ripe peaches, pears, and apples, are good, for these introduce into the system citrates, malates, and other salts of vegetable acids which, by becoming changed into alkaline carbonates in the blood, tend to check undue acidity of the system and to clear and purify the blood.

The danger of these fruits, taken moderately, inducing diarrhœa is more fancied than real.

The chief meal of animal food is best taken at midday, so as to allow of some exercise out of doors afterwards; this, taken a couple of hours or so after the meal, will stimulate the flow of bile into the duodenum just at the time when it is wanted there to digest the oleaginous matters which pass out from the stomach, and the same exercise will also give play to the lungs and thus relieve the liver from being unduly oppressed with the carboniferous elements of the food which it has to convert into bile.

When, of necessity, the chief meal of animal food must come very late in the day, alcoholic stimulants should be used sparingly, and two hours after the dinner tea should be taken, for this, unlike alcohol, promotes the elimination of carbonic acid from the lungs and so aids the latter part of the digestive act. After such a late meal, before finally retiring, a glass of Seltzer, or Fachingen water will be of service to correct and remove any acidity remaining as a result of slow or imperfect action of the digestive organs and when the heart is feeble a little brandy added will ensure a good night's rest.

With respect to the drink taken at meals, there are but few consumptives who do not eat and digest the better for the use of some amount of stimulant with their meals; those who find digestion to proceed better without the aid of stimulants, most certainly should avoid them and take water, or toast and water, with their meals.

For one who is able to eat freely of meat at his chief meal, and take exercise afterwards, good stout or, in some cases Burton ale, will be a nutritious, and not unduly exciting drink, and in this case the patient should keep to plain bread and meat; soups, and much of vegetable or farinaceous food being avoided. The patient thus dieted, and using plenty of exercise at the same time, will be following the beef steak and porter plan of treatment so largely and successfully pursued many years ago by Dr. Stewart of Erskine in cases of consumption.

Those with whom malt liquors do not agree, but who digest better with the aid of some stimulant, should take sherry, weak brandy and water, or such a drink as claret or burgundy, alone or mixed with water; after the meal, either of these two last wines or good port wine may often be allowed with benefit. In hot seasons some persons may find the light white wines of Germany, of Hungary, or of Austria, to agree better than the red, and such experiments as have been made tend to shew that these white wines tend to augment excretion, while the red wines, and especially the Bordeaux wines, retard waste of tissue and check excretion.

To debar the patient from all forms of alcohol seems good only in certain cases to be hereafter alluded to, for practical experience points decidedly to the value of alcohol to the majority of the phthisical.

Taken in moderation it aids the digestive process, and further than this it supplies carbon to the system, in a state apt for oxidation, thus saving too rapid and undue waste of tissue.

Dr. Flint, in his account of 24 cases of arrest of phthisis by simple dietetic and hygienic treatment, while noting the value of a free and liberal diet, comes also most unhesitatingly to the conviction that wine, beer, and spirits, not only aided the digestive process but also seemed in a marked way to check the progress of the disease.

The numerous, but sad cases, that are recorded of individuals who in early youth have been tuberculous, but who have nevertheless lived to become drunkards and to die in old age of delirium tremens, prove strongly the value of alcohol as preventive and curative of consumption.* My own belief is that the Scylla into which these unhappy people fall is worse than the Charybdis they avoid, and that it is better to die in early youth of consumption than to live a life of tippling and die in old age of delirium tremens, or of some chronic disease of the brain, the result of alcoholic poisoning. Happily however, to obtain the good effects of alcohol in phthisis there is no need to bring our patients even within sight of the abyss of intemperance.

The limits of these pages prevent my going further in illustration of the preventive effect of alcohol over phthisis. Used moderately it will do much good in cases where the signs of exhaustion are marked, it will tranquillize the nervous excitement of debility and so check excessive waste of tissue, and taken in moderation at meals it will aid in the digestion and assimilation of food, especially of cod liver oil and fat generally. Never should it be taken in any form on an empty stomach, for then it will cause thickening and induration of the cellular tissue of the stomach walls, and eventually induration and cirrhosis of the liver.

With respect to the form of alcohol to be used, a word more may be said. Rum is, of spirits, the best,

---

* *Incidit in Scyllam qui vult vitare Charybdin.* For one instance see the case of Keith who died of alcoholic mania in the Edinburgh Infirmary at the age of 50, having been at the age of 23 given over to die of consumption. A large cicatrix in the right lung shewed the process of cure that had taken place. Hughes Bennett's *Practice of Medicine*, p. 719, 3rd Edit.

provided the liver be in good and healthy action; Dr. E. Smith has shewn that rum has great power of increasing the exhalation of carbonic acid gas by the lungs, differing notably in this respect from brandy and other alcoholic fluids: hence theory inclines us to advise the use of rum, and the practical experience of patients is that rum taken with water, or on waking in the morning with milk, is a drink of sovereign virtue in quieting cough and relieving great exhaustion.

Dr. Kempt has seen such great benefit arise to the phthisical from the use of rum that he has written a paper on rum as a cure for consumption.

Passing to non-alcoholic fluids, we find in tea a drink, which, like rum, causes a free elimination of carbonic acid from the lungs (Dr. E. Smith) and it is a drink on which a word may be said.

Tea is best taken two or three hours after the chief meal of the day, it then promotes the digestive process, eliminates excess of carbonic acid by the lungs and acts also on the liver and kidneys.

Where the habit is to take a full meal late in the day, tea should be preferred to coffee for breakfast on the next morning.

Dr. E. Smith finds a large cup of cold tea very useful to relieve the profuse night sweats of phthisis, here it gives relief by promoting more free exhalation of carbonic acid by the lungs and more complete oxygenation of the blood.

I find, as matter of experience, that a cup of milk taken at intervals during the night is also a powerful agent in reducing night sweats, and is preferred by some patients to the tea.

Coffee, a drink containing an essential oil, is more suitable to some hysteric and nervous temperaments than tea.

Cocoa, is a nutritious non-stimulating drink much used by invalids; and taken for breakfast, or for lunch, with plenty of milk and sugar it is admirably adapted for phthisical invalids. For those of very delicate digestion Schweitzer's "Cocoatina" is preferable to ordinary Cocoa being remarkably easy of digestion as well as highly nutritious.

In milk we have all the most important elements of nutrition, the saccharine, azotized, and the fatty, well blended together, and as a general rule the more milk a phthisical patient will take the better.

In some few cases, with irregular action of the liver, milk, in every form seems to disagree and is often vomited in the shape of hard lumpy curd. Here it may be tried mixed with an equal part of lime or soda water, but even this admixture does not always enable the stomach to digest it. Donkey's milk forms a light nutritious food for children who are disposed to consumptive disease.

Some are able to take fresh cream with pleasure and benefit, but I believe in the majority of cases skimmed milk will agree, and be digested, better, than any other form and may be very freely given by night, as well as by day, in small quantities at a time to check excessive sweating. The skim milk, as well as new milk, can be taken with one or two table-spoonfuls of rum on first waking in the morning, it will relieve the exhaustion so often felt at that time, and will prevent that undue excitement of the pulse which Dr. E. Smith has shewn always to occur when the consumptive patient rises early without taking a little nourishment first.

Milk, made into a more or less consistent jelly by the addition of Carragheen or Iceland moss, is highly nutritious, and soothing to an irritable mucous membrane; hence where there is tendency to diarrhœa this jelly will be found useful.

The Carragheen moss should be soaked for ten minutes in cold water and then to 24ozs. of milk may be added 1½ drachms of Irish moss, ½oz of loaf sugar, and 1 scruple of Canella or Cinnamon; this mixture should be boiled till it becomes thick and when cold it will be about the consistence of cream. By adding more of the moss a firmer jelly is obtained. In the Danish Pharmacopœia the proportions given for Carragheen-mos-Gelée are 2 drachms of moss to 12ozs. of milk.

The British Pharmacopœia gives as the proportions for the decoction of Iceland moss lichen; moss 1 part; water 30 parts; boil for ten minutes and strain.

Mr. Squire recommends for a pure jelly of this moss:

Iceland moss 1 part; water 10 parts; boil down to 6 parts, strain and add sugar 2 parts. The resulting compounds are demulcent and nutritious and well adapted for cases of debility with pulmonary or gastro-intestinal irritation.

The whey of milk, apart from the curd or casein, is well-known as an article of diet for the phthisical, and has the just credit of having worked cures.

The Prussian Pharmacopœia gives directions for preparing three kinds of whey as follows:

1. An ounce of the dried stomach of the calf is infused with six fluid ounces of cold water for twelve hours. One ounce of this liquor may be added to nine pounds of fresh cow's milk, the mixture gently warmed, and the whey then strained off.

2. Boil three pounds of milk and add one drachm of cream of tartar; when the coagulation is complete strain off the sour whey and boil with some white of egg beaten to a froth until the albumen is coagulated, strain the whey from this and neutralize its acidity with prepared chalk.

By using a drachm of powdered alum in place of the cream of tartar an astringent alum whey is produced, useful in cases of hæmoptysis and diarrhœa.

Where the diet consists chiefly of milk and eggs such farinaceous food as arrowroot, corn-flour, oswego and the like, may be advantageously associated with it, and at times when the patient is kept much at home from hæmoptysis or diarrhœa an exclusive diet of that description of food may be advisable and indeed necessary; the effect of such a light diet in quieting the circulation, arresting hæmoptysis 'or diarrhœa, and relieving congestion of the liver, is often very satisfactory, the patient at the same time partially or entirely giving up all stimulants. By taking beef tea and broths thickened with biscuit powder, the patient may gradually return to the use of animal food.

To lay down precise rules as to the amount of animal food, of alcohol, or of milk, to be taken per day is impossible. Some will do best with but one meal of animal food, while others, and especially those who are young and growing, do better with two, or even three, serves of animal diet.

Whether the chief food be fleshy or farinaceous, fat and butter should enter largely into it for the reasons already given; sugar too is of value as a respiratory food, provided it does not generate acidity of stomach.

In cases of blood-spitting a special plan of diet is essential. Every form and kind of alcohol, I am convinced should, except under urgent need of its administration, to avert death, be withheld. Animal diet in the solid form should be laid aside and the patient fed with milk, eggs, and farinaceous food, till all signs of active bleeding have ceased. Iced water, acidulous drinks, alum whey, toast and water, and tea with slices of lemon in it, are the best drinks under these circumstances for the patient.

In cases of advancing phthisis where the night sweats are profuse and exhausting, associated often too with troublesome diarrhœa, it is of no use to keep the patient to regular meals; he must be fed often during the day, and at intervals during the night also. The food must be varied; eggs with milk, or with wine or brandy, light animal jellies and nutritious soups, thickened perhaps with sago or tapioca or biscuit powder, skimmed milk, and milk with lime water, soda water, or with Iceland or Irish moss, being the chief dietary resources for an invalid in these trying times. The feeding at night with skimmed milk or with cold tea, removal of superfluous coverings, and proper ventilation of the bed rooms are highly important means to check the exhausting sweats as well as greatly to promote the general comfort of the invalid.

By following out the directions and suggestions I have now given, and the inestimable value of which I have proved over and over again, we not only add to our patient's comfort, but at the same time we are doing much to promote renewal of strength and vigour, instead of resorting to the, pardonable perhaps, but unhappy and injurious practice of flying at once to drugs to meet the varied exigencies of the consumptive state.

Wo may be quite certain that there is not the slightest attempt at true rocovery going on while a patient is taking an opiate mixture for the relief of cough, with pills of acotate of lead, or of tannin and opium, to check blood spitting or diarrhœa. The first, oven if it doos for a time impose silence on a troublesome cough, is almost sure at the same time to destroy what little appetite tho patient may possess, and the two last by their sedative and highly astringent properties are eminently adapted to check all secretion of gastric juice and thereby perfectly to arrest the digestive process.

If we really are to cure pulmonary consumption we must get out of the old fashioned track of merely treating symptoms by temporary expedients for palliation; we must look at the disease as a constitutional infirmity of nutrition, and deal with it accordingly.

Years ago, consumption was regarded as an inflammatory disorder of the lungs, and was treated by depletion, by sedatives, and by a hot and humid climate; or else the unfortunate victim was smothered in a hot close room into which no breath of air could enter, and in which the flowers, brought by kind friends, rapidly withered and perished under the overpowering atmosphere; hot and heavy, and polluted by the exhalations from the ulcerated lungs of the invalid. No wonder that under this method of treatment consumption was indeed a deadly and universally fatal disease. Now and then an extraordinary case would be heard of in the instance of one, who, intolerant of this fatal regime, would set doctors, nurses, and friends, at defiance, and go out fishing, shooting, or riding, in all weathers; such an one would be denounced as a madman, and in all probability would live to be an old grey headed man somewhat disposed at times to indulge in a little merriment at the expense of the "Faculty" and their prognostications.

It is hardly necessary for me to remind the reader how already we have begun to treat the disease on principles entirely different to those of our ancestors, and as far as we can at present judge it seems that the duration of life with the consumptive is about double its former duration, a matter both of encouragement and of promise.

The scope of this little book does not admit of more than these general hints and remarks on diet; the great thing to be remembered is, that in curing a disease of mal-nutrition like phthisis we must make diet, air, and exercise, go hand in hand if we are to do the patient good. The first two of these great means of nature's cure have been already discussed, and little more need be said of exercise, save that the patient should not go out fasting, nor directly after food, he should avoid wet, and night air, and then he will do well to be as much out of doors as possible. Walking, riding on horseback, with due care to keep the extremities warm, gentle rowing in a boat, or riding in an open carriage are all means of varying the out door exercise.

When wet weather obliges the invalid to remain in doors, he should not remain too long in one room, he should exercise his arms, and so promote full and deep inspiration, by the use of dumb bells or a hand swing, or he may try the newly-invented India rubber "Gymnast" of Mr. Hodges, a very simple contrivance easily adapted to strong or weak people as a means for the varied exercise of all the limbs.

In all forms of exercise excess of fatigue is to be carefully avoided, and early retirement to rest is advisable with early rising in the morning; care being taken to administer food of some kind equally early in the day.

Where there is tendency to night perspirations, these may be in a degree mitigated by taking sleep during the day and rather less at night, for day sleep Dr. E. Smith finds not to depress the pulse so much as night sleep, and the depression of the pulse at night is one great cause of the exhausting sweats. Food late at night, and in the night, by keeping the pulse more in proper ratio to the respiration, also prevents sweating, as has been already stated.

Attention to the functions of the skin by external bathing, warm, or cold, according to the constitutional vigour and power of reaction of the individual, is very necessary, and the occasional use of the Turkish bath I have found of great use, in the early stages of phthisical disease; moderation in its use is to be inculcated, for some finding great relief are apt to resort to this bath too much till it becomes actually debilitating to the system.

Used with proper precaution the Turkish bath is a most valuable remedial agent in chronic phthisis. It eliminates noxious matters from the blood and prevents their deposition on the lungs. A case recorded some years ago by Dr. Leared, in the Lancet, proves most convincingly the actual curative power of this form of bath in true phthisis.

While the Turkish bath is resorted to at intervals, varying in frequency with the individual requirements of each case, and where our object is powerfully to excite action on the part of the skin and so to relieve embarrassed and oppressed lungs, we must remember to inculcate upon our patients the frequent use of the cold or tepid sponge bath.

A consumptive patient ought every day to have a sponge bath at a temperature of from 60° to 68°, and some sea salt may be added to the water if agreeable.

This bathing process is the most certain preventive that can be adopted to keep off attacks of cold, and to prevent chilliness and shiverings during the day, it will also tend to stimulate the lungs to throw off the phlegm and mucus which has collected in them during the night.

While speaking of this bath and its effects I would wish to say a word on the *feeling of weakness* of which consumptive persons often complain, and that too at a time when every thing shews the physician that a decided turn for the better is being taken.

Thus a patient with a rather hot skin and quick pulse and for whom we have ordered a tepid sponging bath every morning, while admitting that his skin is cooler, his pulse slower, and his rest at night more refreshing, will at the same time express a belief that the bath is weakening him. This is by no means the case, what the patient describes as a feeling of weakness is but the subsidence of that feverish irritation of the system connected with gradually advancing disease, and as the morbid activity ceases there comes over the invalid a sense of calm and rest which he fears is a sign of increasing weakness.

By degrees this feeling passes off and real unmistakeable strength begins to return, provided this natural process of restoration be not frustrated by increased allowance of stimulants or the injudicious administration of tonic medicine. I have myself frequently observed, and it has been remarked to me by my colleague Dr. Peacock, how the patients who are taken into the Victoria Park Hospital, for the first few days of their residence in this institution often complain of feeling weaker; this is because while at home, in circumstances precluding the acquirement of those substantial and nutritious comforts which abound in a well ordered hospital, they were kept in a state of feverish excitement by having a glass of spirits, or a pint of beer, on an empty stomach, they now get, while in the Hospital, milk, cocoa, or beef-tea, instead of a mere stimulant, fever causing, draught, and the sense of rest which the system manifests under this treatment is set down by the patient as weakness, until, a few weeks having passed, a perceptible gain both in weight and strength shews them their error.

It is in the regular use of the tepid, or cold, bath that this illusory feeling of weakness is very apt to distress the patient's mind and cause the abandonment of a very useful curative appliance, hence I have given an explanation of this feeling and shewn whence it springs and why it need not be considered by any means of bad augury.

I have now shewn, to the best of my power, in these pages the curative effect of the powers of the air in pulmonary consumption. As a close confined atmosphere, or one that is at once wet and cold, will assuredly develop the disease in those who are in the least degree disposed thereto, so certainly will a pure clear, dry, and bracing air, prove, in combination with a good and nourishing diet, a remedial agent to which no drug in the Pharmacopœia can be compared for sureness of action.

Hitherto the treatment of consumption by hot rooms, hot climates, bleedings, leechings, and cough mixtures, a practice founded on the most sublime ignorance of the nature and pathology of the disease, has resulted in the death of the patient at no very distant date and the disease has acquired a name for terrible fatality.

By a plan of treatment as opposite as possible to that just described there is not a doubt but that the life of a consumptive patient may be indefinitely prolonged. I can myself point to numerous instances, and we in our profession have the well-known physician Dr. Henry Bennet a standing proof to shew how a wise physician can even heal himself of a disease that we have been taught to believe incurable. Dr. Bennet's method of cure, as given to the world in his small work already referred to, strikingly confirms the truth of the views put forth by the author of these pages.

This book being on the Climatic Treatment of Pulmonary diseases it is not my purpose to add any thing in reference to drugs and their uses in these affections.

It is when we have placed our patient in the most favorable natural conditions for staying the progress of his complaint that we must see what help drugs will give, not only to meet complications as they arise, but actually to promote the curative process.

Cod liver oil, and for a pure uniform reliable oil I know of none superior to that sold as Möller's oil, and Pancreatic emulsion are both food and physic, supplying the stomach with very digestible fat and so enabling the system to obtain this matter in a form easy of assimilation by the tissues, a point of the greatest importance.

Some patients do best with the oil, or the emulsion immediately after meals—others at an interval of an hour or two. Often it is a good plan to take a dose of the cod-liver oil the very last thing at night, it quiets the cough and tends to check night sweating and prevents feeling of excessive exhaustion on waking in the morning.

Further than this in the matter of drug treatment it is not my purpose to go; I am myself no believer in the invention of "a specific" that is to cure all forms of phthisis, but at the same time experience teaches me to place great confidence in a judicious well applied method of drug treatment as promoting not only the comfort, but the actual cure of consumptive persons. The misfortune is, that our patients commonly rely far too exclusively on mere physic and will swallow anything in the way of physic, be it new or old, rather than attend to the imperative conditions which nature points out as the first step towards their real and permanent cure.

And thus it is that we so often see the consumptive invalid going from one physician to another and taking abundance of cod-liver oil, with tonic, sedative, expectorant, and astringent mixtures, useful and good enough in their way, but on no account to be regarded as the only means by which phthisis is to be arrested, for the legitimate sphere of such remedial measures as these is in reality quite secondary and subordinate to those powerful and efficient means of prevention and cure which nature offers to the invalid in the shape of fresh air, proper food, and free exercise.

THE END.

www.ingramcontent.com/pod-product-compliance
Lightning Source LLC
Chambersburg PA
CBHW020146170426
43199CB00010B/916